The Law School Admission Council (LSAC) is a nonprofit corporation that provides unique, state-of-the-art admission products and services to ease the admission process for law schools and their applicants worldwide. More than 200 law schools in the United States, Canada, and Australia are members of the Council and benefit from LSAC's services.

LSAC fees, policies, and procedures relating to, but not limited to, test registration, test administration, test score reporting, misconduct and irregularities, Credential Assembly Service (CAS), and other matters may change without notice at any time. Up-to-date LSAC policies and procedures are available at LSAC.org, or you may contact our candidate service representatives.

ISBN-13: 978-0-9821487-7-8
ISBN-10: 0-9821487-7-1

TABLE OF CONTENTS

The Law School Admission Test is a half-day standardized test required for admission to all ABA-approved law schools, most Canadian law schools, and many other law schools. It consists of five 35-minute sections of multiple-choice questions. Four of the five sections contribute to the test taker's score. These sections include one reading comprehension section, one analytical reasoning section, and two logical reasoning sections. The unscored section, commonly referred to as the variable section, typically is used to pretest new test questions or to preequate new test forms. The placement of this section in the LSAT will vary. A 35-minute writing sample is administered at the end of the test. The writing sample is not scored by LSAC, but copies are sent to all law schools to which you apply. The score scale for the LSAT is 120 to 180.

The LSAT is designed to measure skills considered essential for success in law school: the reading and comprehension of complex texts with accuracy and insight; the organization and management of information and the ability to draw reasonable inferences from it; the ability to think critically; and the analysis and evaluation of the reasoning and arguments of others.

The LSAT provides a standard measure of acquired reading and verbal reasoning skills that law schools can use as one of several factors in assessing applicants.

For up-to-date information about LSAC's services, go to our website, LSAC.org.

SCORING

Your LSAT score is based on the number of questions you answer correctly (the raw score). There is no deduction for incorrect answers, and all questions count equally. In other words, there is no penalty for guessing.

Test Score Accuracy—Reliability and Standard Error of Measurement

Candidates perform at different levels on different occasions for reasons quite unrelated to the characteristics of a test itself. The accuracy of test scores is best described by the use of two related statistical terms: reliability and standard error of measurement.

Reliability is a measure of how consistently a test measures the skills being assessed. The higher the reliability coefficient for a test, the more certain we can be that test takers would get very similar scores if they took the test again.

LSAC reports an internal consistency measure of reliability for every test form. Reliability can vary from 0.00 to 1.00, and a test with no measurement error would have a reliability coefficient of 1.00 (never attained in practice). Reliability coefficients for past LSAT forms have ranged from .90 to .95, indicating a high degree of consistency for these tests. LSAC expects the reliability of the LSAT to continue to fall within the same range.

LSAC also reports the amount of measurement error associated with each test form, a concept known as the standard error of measurement (SEM). The SEM, which is usually about 2.6 points, indicates how close a test taker's observed score is likely to be to his or her true score. True scores are theoretical scores that would be obtained from perfectly reliable tests with no measurement error—scores never known in practice.

Score bands, or ranges of scores that contain a test taker's true score a certain percentage of the time, can be derived using the SEM. LSAT score bands are constructed by adding and subtracting the (rounded) SEM to and from an actual LSAT score (e.g., the LSAT score, plus or minus 3 points). Scores near 120 or 180 have asymmetrical bands. Score bands constructed in this manner will contain an individual's true score approximately 68 percent of the time.

Measurement error also must be taken into account when comparing LSAT scores of two test takers. It is likely that small differences in scores are due to measurement error rather than to meaningful differences in ability. The standard error of score differences provides some guidance as to the importance of differences between two scores. The standard error of score differences is approximately 1.4 times larger than the standard error of measurement for the individual scores.

Thus, a test score should be regarded as a useful but approximate measure of a test taker's abilities as measured by the test, not as an exact determination of his or her abilities. LSAC encourages law schools to examine the range of scores within the interval that probably contains the test taker's true score (e.g., the test taker's score band) rather than solely interpret the reported score alone.

Adjustments for Variation in Test Difficulty

All test forms of the LSAT reported on the same score scale are designed to measure the same abilities, but one test form may be slightly easier or more difficult than another. The scores from different test forms are made comparable through a statistical procedure known as equating. As a result of equating, a given scaled score earned on different test forms reflects the same level of ability.

Research on the LSAT

Summaries of LSAT validity studies and other LSAT research can be found in member law school libraries and at LSAC.org.

To Inquire About Test Questions

If you find what you believe to be an error or ambiguity in a test question that affects your response to the question, contact LSAC by e-mail: LSATTS@LSAC.org, or write to Law School Admission Council, Test Development Group, Box 40, Newtown, PA 18940-0040.

HOW THIS PREPTEST DIFFERS FROM AN ACTUAL LSAT

This PrepTest is made up of the scored sections and writing sample from the actual disclosed LSAT administered in October 2010. However, it does not contain the extra, variable section that is used to pretest new test items of one of the three multiple-choice question types. The three multiple-choice question types may be in a different order in an actual LSAT than in this PrepTest. This is because the order of these question types is intentionally varied for each administration of the test.

THE THREE LSAT MULTIPLE-CHOICE QUESTION TYPES

The multiple-choice questions that make up most of the LSAT reflect a broad range of academic disciplines and are intended to give no advantage to candidates from a particular academic background.

The five sections of the test contain three different question types. The following material presents a general discussion of the nature of each question type and some strategies that can be used in answering them.

Analytical Reasoning Questions

Analytical Reasoning questions are designed to assess the ability to consider a group of facts and rules, and, given those facts and rules, determine what could or must be true. The specific scenarios associated with these questions are usually unrelated to law, since they are intended to be accessible to a wide range of test takers. However, the skills tested parallel those involved in determining what could or must be the case given a set of regulations, the terms of a contract, or the facts of a legal case in relation to the law. In Analytical Reasoning questions, you are asked to reason deductively from a set of statements and rules or principles that describe relationships among persons, things, or events.

Analytical Reasoning questions appear in sets, with each set based on a single passage. The passage used for each set of questions describes common ordering relationships or grouping relationships, or a combination of both types of relationships. Examples include scheduling employees for work shifts, assigning instructors to class sections, ordering tasks according to priority, and distributing grants for projects.

Analytical Reasoning questions test a range of deductive reasoning skills. These include:

- Comprehending the basic structure of a set of relationships by determining a complete solution to the problem posed (for example, an acceptable seating arrangement of all six diplomats around a table)

- Reasoning with conditional ("if-then") statements and recognizing logically equivalent formulations of such statements

- Inferring what could be true or must be true from given facts and rules

- Inferring what could be true or must be true from given facts and rules together with new information in the form of an additional or substitute fact or rule

- Recognizing when two statements are logically equivalent in context by identifying a condition or rule that could replace one of the original conditions while still resulting in the same possible outcomes

Analytical Reasoning questions reflect the kinds of detailed analyses of relationships and sets of constraints that a law student must perform in legal problem solving. For example, an Analytical Reasoning passage might describe six diplomats being seated around a table, following certain rules of protocol as to who can sit where. You, the test taker, must answer questions about the logical implications of given and new information. For example, you may be asked who can sit between diplomats X and Y, or who cannot sit next to X if W sits next to Y. Similarly, if you were a student in law school, you might be asked to analyze a scenario involving a set of particular circumstances and a set of governing rules in the form of constitutional provisions, statutes, administrative codes, or prior rulings that have been upheld. You might then be asked to determine the legal options in the scenario: what is required given the scenario, what is permissible given the scenario, and what is prohibited given the scenario. Or you might be asked to develop a "theory" for the case: when faced with an incomplete set of facts about the case, you must fill in the picture based on what is implied by the facts that are known. The problem could be elaborated by the addition of new information or hypotheticals.

No formal training in logic is required to answer these questions correctly. Analytical Reasoning questions are intended to be answered using knowledge, skills, and reasoning ability generally expected of college students and graduates.

Suggested Approach

Some people may prefer to answer first those questions about a passage that seem less difficult and then those that seem more difficult. In general, it is best to finish one passage before starting on another, because much time can be lost in returning to a passage and reestablishing familiarity with its relationships. However, if you are having great difficulty on one particular set of questions and are spending too much time on them, it may be to your advantage to skip that set of questions and go on to the next passage, returning to the problematic set of questions after you have finished the other questions in the section.

Do not assume that because the conditions for a set of questions look long or complicated, the questions based on those conditions will be especially difficult.

Read the passage carefully. Careful reading and analysis are necessary to determine the exact nature of the relationships involved in an Analytical Reasoning passage. Some relationships are fixed (for example, P and R must always work on the same project). Other relationships are variable (for example, Q must be assigned to either team 1 or team 3). Some relationships that are not stated explicitly in the conditions are implied by and can be deduced from those that are stated (for example, if one condition about paintings in a display specifies that Painting K must be to the left of Painting Y, and another specifies that Painting W must be to the left of Painting K, then it can be deduced that Painting W must be to the left of Painting Y).

In reading the conditions, do not introduce unwarranted assumptions. For instance, in a set of questions establishing relationships of height and weight among the members of a team, do not assume that a person who is taller than another person must weigh more than that person. As another example, suppose a set involves ordering and a question in the set asks what must be true if both X and Y must be earlier than Z; in this case, do not assume that X must be earlier than Y merely because X is mentioned before Y. All the information needed to answer each question is provided in the passage and the question itself.

The conditions are designed to be as clear as possible. Do not interpret the conditions as if they were intended to trick you. For example, if a question asks how many people could be eligible to serve on a committee, consider only those people named in the passage unless directed otherwise. When in doubt, read the conditions in their most obvious sense. Remember, however, that the language in the conditions is intended to be read for precise meaning. It is essential to pay particular attention to words that describe or limit relationships, such as "only," "exactly," "never," "always," "must be," "cannot be," and the like.

The result of this careful reading will be a clear picture of the structure of the relationships involved, including the kinds of relationships permitted, the participants in the relationships, and the range of possible actions or attributes for these participants.

Keep in mind question independence. Each question should be considered separately from the other questions in its set. No information, except what is given in the original conditions, should be carried over from one question to another.

In some cases a question will simply ask for conclusions to be drawn from the conditions as originally given. Some questions may, however, add information to the original conditions or temporarily suspend or replace one of the original conditions for the purpose of that question only. For example, if Question 1 adds the supposition "if P is sitting at table 2 ...," this supposition should NOT be carried over to any other question in the set.

Consider highlighting text and using diagrams. Many people find it useful to underline key points in the passage and in each question. In addition, it may prove very helpful to draw a diagram to assist you in finding the solution to the problem.

In preparing for the test, you may wish to experiment with different types of diagrams. For a scheduling problem, a simple calendar-like diagram may be helpful. For a grouping problem, an array of labeled columns or rows may be useful.

Even though most people find diagrams to be very helpful, some people seldom use them, and for some individual questions no one will need a diagram. There is by no means universal agreement on which kind of diagram is best for which problem or in which cases a diagram is most useful. Do not be concerned if a particular problem in the test seems to be best approached without the use of a diagram.

Logical Reasoning Questions

Arguments are a fundamental part of the law, and analyzing arguments is a key element of legal analysis. Training in the law builds on a foundation of basic reasoning skills. Law students must draw on the skills of analyzing, evaluating, constructing, and refuting arguments. They need to be able to identify what information is relevant to an issue or argument and what impact further evidence might have. They need to be able to reconcile opposing positions and use arguments to persuade others.

Logical Reasoning questions evaluate the ability to analyze, critically evaluate, and complete arguments as they occur in ordinary language. The questions are based on short arguments drawn from a wide variety of sources, including newspapers, general interest magazines, scholarly publications, advertisements, and informal discourse. These arguments mirror legal reasoning in the types of arguments presented and in their complexity, though few of the arguments actually have law as a subject matter.

Each Logical Reasoning question requires you to read and comprehend a short passage, then answer one question (or, rarely, two questions) about it. The questions are designed to assess a wide range of skills involved in thinking critically, with an emphasis on skills that are central to legal reasoning.

These skills include:

- Recognizing the parts of an argument and their relationships

- Recognizing similarities and differences between patterns of reasoning

- Drawing well-supported conclusions

- Reasoning by analogy

- Recognizing misunderstandings or points of disagreement

- Determining how additional evidence affects an argument

- Detecting assumptions made by particular arguments

- Identifying and applying principles or rules

- Identifying flaws in arguments

- Identifying explanations

The questions do not presuppose specialized knowledge of logical terminology. For example, you will not be expected to know the meaning of specialized terms such as "ad hominem" or "syllogism." On the other hand, you will be expected to understand and critique the reasoning contained in arguments. This requires that you possess a university-level understanding of widely used concepts such as argument, premise, assumption, and conclusion.

Suggested Approach

Read each question carefully. Make sure that you understand the meaning of each part of the question. Make sure that you understand the meaning of each answer choice and the ways in which it may or may not relate to the question posed.

Do not pick a response simply because it is a true statement. Although true, it may not answer the question posed.

Answer each question on the basis of the information that is given, even if you do not agree with it. Work within the context provided by the passage. LSAT questions do not involve any tricks or hidden meanings.

Reading Comprehension Questions

Both law school and the practice of law revolve around extensive reading of highly varied, dense, argumentative, and expository texts (for example, cases, codes, contracts, briefs, decisions, evidence). This reading must be exacting, distinguishing precisely what is said from what is not said. It involves comparison, analysis, synthesis, and application (for example, of principles and rules). It involves drawing appropriate inferences and applying ideas and arguments to new contexts. Law school reading also requires the ability to grasp unfamiliar subject matter and the ability to penetrate difficult and challenging material.

The purpose of LSAT Reading Comprehension questions is to measure the ability to read, with understanding and insight, examples of lengthy and complex materials similar to those commonly encountered in law school. The Reading Comprehension section of the LSAT contains four sets of reading questions, each set consisting of a selection of reading material followed by five to eight questions. The reading selection in three of the four sets consists of a single reading passage; the other set contains two related shorter passages. Sets with two passages are a variant of Reading Comprehension called Comparative Reading, which was introduced in June 2007.

Comparative Reading questions concern the relationships between the two passages, such as those of generalization/instance, principle/application, or point/counterpoint. Law school work often requires reading two or more texts in conjunction with each other and understanding their relationships. For example, a law student may read a trial court decision together with an appellate court decision that overturns it, or identify the fact pattern from a hypothetical suit together with the potentially controlling case law.

Reading selections for LSAT Reading Comprehension questions are drawn from a wide range of subjects in the humanities, the social sciences, the biological and physical sciences, and areas related to the law. Generally, the selections are densely written, use high-level vocabulary, and contain sophisticated argument or complex rhetorical structure (for example, multiple points of view). Reading Comprehension questions require you to read carefully and accurately, to determine the relationships among the various parts of the reading selection, and to draw reasonable inferences from the material in the selection. The questions may ask about the following characteristics of a passage or pair of passages:

- The main idea or primary purpose

- Information that is explicitly stated

- Information or ideas that can be inferred

- The meaning or purpose of words or phrases as used in context

- The organization or structure

- The application of information in the selection to a new context

- Principles that function in the selection

- Analogies to claims or arguments in the selection

- An author's attitude as revealed in the tone of a passage or the language used

- The impact of new information on claims or arguments in the selection

Suggested Approach

Since reading selections are drawn from many different disciplines and sources, you should not be discouraged if you encounter material with which you are not familiar. It is important to remember that questions are to be answered exclusively on the basis of the information provided in the selection. There is no particular knowledge that you are expected to bring to the test, and you should not make inferences based on any prior knowledge of a subject that you may have. You may, however, wish to defer working on a set of questions that seems particularly difficult or unfamiliar until after you have dealt with sets you find easier.

Strategies. One question that often arises in connection with Reading Comprehension has to do with the most effective and efficient order in which to read the selections and questions. Possible approaches include:

- reading the selection very closely and then answering the questions;

- reading the questions first, reading the selection closely, and then returning to the questions; or

- skimming the selection and questions very quickly, then rereading the selection closely and answering the questions.

Test takers are different, and the best strategy for one might not be the best strategy for another. In preparing for the test, therefore, you might want to experiment with the different strategies and decide what works most effectively for you.

Remember that your strategy must be effective under timed conditions. For this reason, the first strategy—reading the selection very closely and then answering the questions—may be the most effective for you. Nonetheless, if you believe that one of the other strategies

might be more effective for you, you should try it out and assess your performance using it.

Reading the selection. Whatever strategy you choose, you should give the passage or pair of passages at least one careful reading before answering the questions. Try to distinguish main ideas from supporting ideas, and opinions or attitudes from factual, objective information. Note transitions from one idea to the next and identify the relationships among the different ideas or parts of a passage, or between the two passages in comparative reading sets. Consider how and why an author makes points and draws conclusions. Be sensitive to implications of what the passages say.

You may find it helpful to mark key parts of passages. For example, you might underline main ideas or important arguments, and you might circle transitional words—"although," "nevertheless," "correspondingly," and the like—that will help you map the structure of a passage. Also, you might note descriptive words that will help you identify an author's attitude toward a particular idea or person.

Answering the Questions

- Always read all the answer choices before selecting the best answer. The best answer choice is the one that most accurately and completely answers the question being posed.

- Respond to the specific question being asked. Do not pick an answer choice simply because it is a true statement. For example, picking a true statement might yield an incorrect answer to a question in which you are asked to identify an author's position on an issue, since you are not being asked to evaluate the truth of the author's position but only to correctly identify what that position is.

- Answer the questions only on the basis of the information provided in the selection. Your own views, interpretations, or opinions, and those you have heard from others, may sometimes conflict with those expressed in a reading selection; however, you are expected to work within the context provided by the reading selection. You should not expect to agree with everything you encounter in reading comprehension passages.

THE WRITING SAMPLE

On the day of the test, you will be asked to write one sample essay. LSAC does not score the writing sample, but copies are sent to all law schools to which you apply. According to a 2006 LSAC survey of 157 United States and Canadian law schools, almost all use the writing sample in evaluating at least some applications for admission. Failure to respond to writing sample prompts and frivolous responses have been used by law schools as grounds for rejection of applications for admission.

In developing and implementing the writing sample portion of the LSAT, LSAC has operated on the following premises: First, law schools and the legal profession value highly the ability to communicate effectively in writing. Second, it is important to encourage potential law students to develop effective writing skills. Third, a sample of an applicant's writing, produced under controlled conditions, is a potentially useful indication of that person's writing ability. Fourth, the writing sample can serve as an independent check on other writing submitted by applicants as part of the admission process. Finally, writing samples may be useful for diagnostic purposes related to improving a candidate's writing.

The writing prompt presents a decision problem. You are asked to make a choice between two positions or courses of action. Both of the choices are defensible, and you are given criteria and facts on which to base your decision. There is no "right" or "wrong" position to take on the topic, so the quality of each test taker's response is a function not of which choice is made, but of how well or poorly the choice is supported and how well or poorly the other choice is criticized.

The LSAT writing prompt was designed and validated by legal education professionals. Since it involves writing based on fact sets and criteria, the writing sample gives applicants the opportunity to demonstrate the type of argumentative writing that is required in law school, although the topics are usually nonlegal.

You will have 35 minutes in which to plan and write an essay on the topic you receive. Read the topic and the accompanying directions carefully. You will probably find it best to spend a few minutes considering the topic and organizing your thoughts before you begin writing. In your essay, be sure to develop your ideas fully, leaving time, if possible, to review what you have written. Do not write on a topic other than the one specified. Writing on a topic of your own choice is not acceptable.

No special knowledge is required or expected for this writing exercise. Law schools are interested in the reasoning, clarity, organization, language usage, and writing mechanics displayed in your essay. How well you write is more important than how much you write. Confine your essay to the blocked, lined area on the front and back of the separate Writing Sample Response Sheet. Only that area will be reproduced for law schools. Be sure that your writing is legible.

TAKING THE PREPTEST UNDER SIMULATED LSAT CONDITIONS

One important way to prepare for the LSAT is to simulate the day of the test by taking a practice test under actual time constraints. Taking a practice test under timed conditions helps you to estimate the amount of time you can afford to spend on each question in a section and to determine the question types on which you may need additional practice.

Since the LSAT is a timed test, it is important to use your allotted time wisely. During the test, you may work only on the section designated by the test supervisor. You can-not devote extra time to a difficult section and make up that time on a section you find easier. In pacing yourself, and checking your answers, you should think of each section of the test as a separate minitest.

Be sure that you answer every question on the test. When you do not know the correct answer to a question, first eliminate the responses that you know are incorrect, then make your best guess among the remaining choices. Do not be afraid to guess as there is no penalty for incorrect answers.

When you take a practice test, abide by all the requirements specified in the directions and keep strictly within the specified time limits. Work without a rest period. When you take an actual test, you will have only a short break—usually 10–15 minutes—after SECTION III.

When taken under conditions as much like actual testing conditions as possible, a practice test provides very useful preparation for taking the LSAT.

Official directions for the four multiple-choice sections and the writing sample are included in this PrepTest so that you can approximate actual testing conditions as you practice.

To take the test:

- Set a timer for 35 minutes. Answer all the questions in SECTION I of this PrepTest. Stop working on that section when the 35 minutes have elapsed.

- Repeat, allowing yourself 35 minutes each for sections II, III, and IV.

- Set the timer again for 35 minutes, then prepare your response to the writing sample topic at the end of this PrepTest.

- Refer to "Computing Your Score" for the PrepTest for instruction on evaluating your performance. An answer key is provided for that purpose.

The practice test that follows consists of four sections corresponding to the four scored sections of the October 2010 LSAT. Also reprinted is the October 2010 unscored writing sample topic.

General Directions for the LSAT Answer Sheet

The actual testing time for this portion of the test will be 2 hours 55 minutes. There are five sections, each with a time limit of 35 minutes. The supervisor will tell you when to begin and end each section. If you finish a section before time is called, you may check your work on that section <u>only</u>; do not turn to any other section of the test book and do not work on any other section either in the test book or on the answer sheet.

There are several different types of questions on the test, and each question type has its own directions. <u>Be sure you understand the directions for each question type before attempting to answer any questions in that section.</u>

Not everyone will finish all the questions in the time allowed. Do not hurry, but work steadily and as quickly as you can without sacrificing accuracy. You are advised to use your time effectively. If a question seems too difficult, go on to the next one and return to the difficult question after completing the section. MARK THE BEST ANSWER YOU CAN FOR EVERY QUESTION. NO DEDUCTIONS WILL BE MADE FOR WRONG ANSWERS. YOUR SCORE WILL BE BASED ONLY ON THE NUMBER OF QUESTIONS YOU ANSWER CORRECTLY.

ALL YOUR ANSWERS MUST BE MARKED ON THE ANSWER SHEET. Answer spaces for each question are lettered to correspond with the letters of the potential answers to each question in the test book. After you have decided which of the answers is correct, blacken the corresponding space on the answer sheet. BE SURE THAT EACH MARK IS BLACK AND COMPLETELY FILLS THE ANSWER SPACE. Give only one answer to each question. If you change an answer, be sure that all previous marks are <u>erased completely</u>. Since the answer sheet is machine scored, incomplete erasures may be interpreted as intended answers. ANSWERS RECORDED IN THE TEST BOOK WILL NOT BE SCORED.

There may be more questions noted on this answer sheet than there are questions in a section. Do not be concerned but be certain that the section and number of the question you are answering matches the answer sheet section and question number. Additional answer spaces in any answer sheet section should be left blank. Begin your next section in the number one answer space for that section.

LSAC takes various steps to ensure that answer sheets are returned from test centers in a timely manner for processing. In the unlikely event that an answer sheet(s) is not received, LSAC will permit the examinee to either retest at no additional fee or to receive a refund of his or her LSAT fee. THESE REMEDIES ARE THE EXCLUSIVE REMEDIES AVAILABLE IN THE UNLIKELY EVENT THAT AN ANSWER SHEET IS NOT RECEIVED BY LSAC.

Score Cancellation

Complete this section only if you are absolutely certain you want to cancel your score. A CANCELLATION REQUEST CANNOT BE RESCINDED. IF YOU ARE AT ALL UNCERTAIN, YOU SHOULD <u>NOT</u> COMPLETE THIS SECTION.

To cancel your score from this administration, you **must**:

A. fill in both ovals here ..... ○ ○
   AND

B. read the following statement. Then sign your name and enter the date.
   YOUR SIGNATURE ALONE IS NOT SUFFICIENT FOR SCORE CANCELLATION. BOTH OVALS ABOVE MUST BE FILLED IN FOR SCANNING EQUIPMENT TO RECOGNIZE YOUR REQUEST FOR SCORE CANCELLATION.

I certify that I wish to cancel my test score from this administration. I understand that my request is irreversible and that my score will not be sent to me or to the law schools to which I apply.

_____
Sign your name in full

_____
Date

FOR LSAC USE ONLY

HOW DID YOU PREPARE FOR THE LSAT?
(Select all that apply.)

Responses to this item are voluntary and will be used for statistical research purposes only.

○ By studying the free sample questions available on LSAC's website.
○ By taking the free sample LSAT available on LSAC's website.
○ By working through official LSAT *PrepTests*, *ItemWise*, and/or other LSAC test prep products.
○ By using LSAT prep books or software **not** published by LSAC.
○ By attending a commercial test preparation or coaching course.
○ By attending a test preparation or coaching course offered through an undergraduate institution.
○ Self study.
○ Other preparation.
○ No preparation.

CERTIFYING STATEMENT

Please write the following statement. Sign and date.

I certify that I am the examinee whose name appears on this answer sheet and that I am here to take the LSAT for the sole purpose of being considered for admission to law school. I further certify that I will neither assist nor receive assistance from any other candidate, and I agree not to copy or retain examination questions or to transmit them to or discuss them with any other person in any form.

_____
_____
_____
_____
_____
_____
_____
_____

SIGNATURE: _____ TODAY'S DATE: ___/___/___
                                                      MONTH DAY YEAR

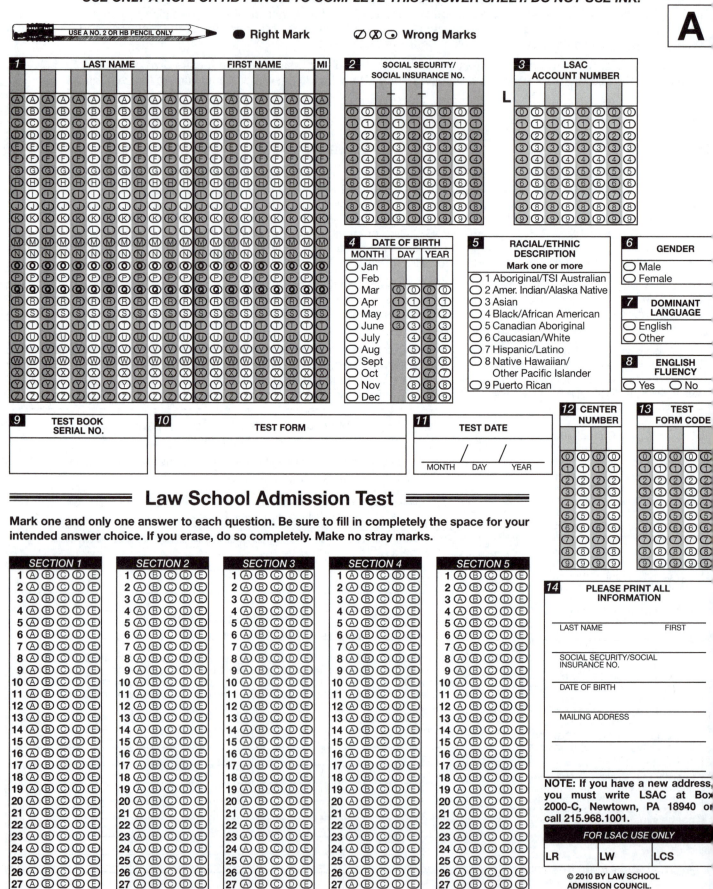

THE PREPTEST

SECTION I

Time—35 minutes

27 Questions

Directions: Each set of questions in this section is based on a single passage or a pair of passages. The questions are to be answered on the basis of what is stated or implied in the passage or pair of passages. For some of the questions, more than one of the choices could conceivably answer the question. However, you are to choose the best answer; that is, the response that most accurately and completely answers the question, and blacken the corresponding space on your answer sheet.

The Universal Declaration of Human Rights (UDHR), approved by the United Nations General Assembly in 1948, was the first international treaty to expressly affirm universal respect for human rights.
(5) Prior to 1948 no truly international standard of humanitarian beliefs existed. Although Article 1 of the 1945 UN Charter had been written with the express purpose of obligating the UN to "encourage respect for human rights and for fundamental
(10) freedoms for all without distinction as to race, sex, language, or religion," there were members of delegations from various small countries and representatives of several nongovernmental organizations who felt that the language of Article 1
(15) was not strong enough, and that the Charter as a whole did not go far enough in its efforts to guarantee basic human rights. This group lobbied vigorously to strengthen the Charter's human rights provisions and proposed that member states be
(20) required "to take separate and joint action and to co-operate with the organization for the promotion of human rights." This would have implied an obligation for member states to act on human rights issues. Ultimately, this proposal and others like it were not
(25) adopted; instead, the UDHR was commissioned and drafted.

The original mandate for producing the document was given to the UN Commission on Human Rights in February 1946. Between that time and the General
(30) Assembly's final approval of the document, the UDHR passed through an elaborate eight-stage drafting process in which it made its way through almost every level of the UN hierarchy. The articles were debated at each stage, and all 30 articles were
(35) argued passionately by delegates representing diverse ideologies, traditions, and cultures. The document as it was finally approved set forth the essential principles of freedom and equality for everyone— regardless of sex, race, color, language, religion,
(40) political or other opinion, national or social origin, property, birth or other status. It also asserted a number of fundamental human rights, including among others the right to work, the right to rest and leisure, and the right to education.
(45) While the UDHR is in many ways a progressive document, it also has weaknesses, the most regrettable of which is its nonbinding legal status. For all its strong language and high ideals, the UDHR remains a resolution of a purely programmatic nature.
(50) Nevertheless, the document has led, even if belatedly, to the creation of legally binding human rights

conventions, and it clearly deserves recognition as an international standard-setting piece of work, as a set of aspirations to which UN member states are
(55) intended to strive, and as a call to arms in the name of humanity, justice, and freedom.

1. By referring to the Universal Declaration of Human Rights as "purely programmatic" (line 49) in nature, the author most likely intends to emphasize

(A) the likelihood that the document will inspire innovative government programs designed to safeguard human rights
(B) the ability of the document's drafters to translate abstract ideals into concrete standards
(C) the compromises that went into producing a version of the document that would garner the approval of all relevant parties
(D) the fact that the guidelines established by the document are ultimately unenforceable
(E) the frustration experienced by the document's drafters at stubborn resistance from within the UN hierarchy

2. The author most probably quotes directly from both the UN Charter (lines 8–11) and the proposal mentioned in lines 20–22 for which one of the following reasons?

(A) to contrast the different definitions of human rights in the two documents
(B) to compare the strength of the human rights language in the two documents
(C) to identify a bureaucratic vocabulary that is common to the two documents
(D) to highlight what the author believes to be the most important point in each document
(E) to call attention to a significant difference in the prose styles of the two documents

3. The author's stance toward the Universal Declaration of Human Rights can best be described as

(A) unbridled enthusiasm
(B) qualified approval
(C) absolute neutrality
(D) reluctant rejection
(E) strong hostility

GO ON TO THE NEXT PAGE.

4. According to the passage, each of the following is true of the Universal Declaration of Human Rights EXCEPT:

(A) It asserts a right to rest and leisure.
(B) It was drafted after the UN Charter was drafted.
(C) The UN Commission on Human Rights was charged with producing it.
(D) It has had no practical consequences.
(E) It was the first international treaty to explicitly affirm universal respect for human rights.

5. The author would be most likely to agree with which one of the following statements?

(A) The human rights language contained in Article 1 of the UN Charter is so ambiguous as to be almost wholly ineffectual.
(B) The weaknesses of the Universal Declaration of Human Rights generally outweigh the strengths of the document.
(C) It was relatively easy for the drafters of the Universal Declaration of Human Rights to reach a consensus concerning the contents of the document.
(D) The drafters of the Universal Declaration of Human Rights omitted important rights that should be included in a truly comprehensive list of basic human rights.
(E) The Universal Declaration of Human Rights would be truer to the intentions of its staunchest proponents if UN member countries were required by law to abide by its provisions.

6. Suppose that a group of independent journalists has uncovered evidence of human rights abuses being perpetrated by a security agency of a UN member state upon a group of political dissidents. Which one of the following approaches to the situation would most likely be advocated by present-day delegates who share the views of the delegates and representatives mentioned in lines 11–14?

(A) The UN General Assembly authenticates the evidence and then insists upon prompt remedial action on the part of the government of the member state.
(B) The UN General Assembly stipulates that any proposed response must be unanimously accepted by member states before it can be implemented.
(C) The UN issues a report critical of the actions of the member state in question and calls for a censure vote in the General Assembly.
(D) The situation is regarded by the UN as an internal matter that is best left to the discretion of the government of the member state.
(E) The situation is investigated further by nongovernmental humanitarian organizations that promise to disclose their findings to the public via the international media.

GO ON TO THE NEXT PAGE.

It is commonly assumed that even if some forgeries have aesthetic merit, no forgery has as much as an original by the imitated artist would. Yet even the most prominent art specialists can be duped by a (5) talented artist turned forger into mistaking an almost perfect forgery for an original. For instance, artist Han van Meegeren's *The Disciples at Emmaus* (1937)—painted under the forged signature of the acclaimed Dutch master Jan Vermeer (1632–1675)— (10) attracted lavish praise from experts as one of Vermeer's finest works. The painting hung in a Rotterdam museum until 1945, when, to the great embarrassment of the critics, van Meegeren revealed its origin. Astonishingly, there was at least one highly (15) reputed critic who persisted in believing it to be a Vermeer even after van Meegeren's confession.

Given the experts' initial enthusiasm, some philosophers argue that van Meegeren's painting must have possessed aesthetic characteristics that, in a (20) Vermeer original, would have justified the critics' plaudits. Van Meegeren's *Emmaus* thus raises difficult questions regarding the status of superbly executed forgeries. Is a forgery inherently inferior as art? How are we justified, if indeed we are, in revising (25) downwards our critical assessment of a work unmasked as a forgery? Philosopher of art Alfred Lessing proposes convincing answers to these questions.

A forged work is indeed inferior as art, Lessing (30) argues, but not because of a shortfall in aesthetic qualities strictly defined, that is to say, in the qualities perceptible on the picture's surface. For example, in its composition, its technique, and its brilliant use of color, van Meegeren's work is flawless, even (35) beautiful. Lessing argues instead that the deficiency lies in what might be called the painting's intangible qualities. All art, explains Lessing, involves technique, but not all art involves origination of a new vision, and originality of vision is one of the (40) fundamental qualities by which artistic, as opposed to purely aesthetic, accomplishment is measured. Thus Vermeer is acclaimed for having inaugurated, in the seventeenth century, a new way of seeing, and for pioneering techniques for embodying this new way of (45) seeing through distinctive treatment of light, color, and form.

Even if we grant that van Meegeren, with his undoubted mastery of Vermeer's innovative techniques, produced an aesthetically superior (50) painting, he did so about three centuries after Vermeer developed the techniques in question. Whereas Vermeer's origination of these techniques in the seventeenth century represents a truly impressive and historic achievement, van Meegeren's production (55) of *The Disciples at Emmaus* in the twentieth century presents nothing new or creative to the history of art. Van Meegeren's forgery therefore, for all its aesthetic merits, lacks the historical significance that makes Vermeer's work artistically great.

7. Which one of the following most accurately expresses the main point of the passage?

(A) *The Disciples at Emmaus*, van Meegeren's forgery of a Vermeer, was a failure in both aesthetic and artistic terms.

(B) The aesthetic value of a work of art is less dependent on the work's visible characteristics than on certain intangible characteristics.

(C) Forged artworks are artistically inferior to originals because artistic value depends in large part on originality of vision.

(D) The most skilled forgers can deceive even highly qualified art experts into accepting their work as original.

(E) Art critics tend to be unreliable judges of the aesthetic and artistic quality of works of art.

8. The passage provides the strongest support for inferring that Lessing holds which one of the following views?

(A) The judgments of critics who pronounced *The Disciples at Emmaus* to be aesthetically superb were not invalidated by the revelation that the painting is a forgery.

(B) The financial value of a work of art depends more on its purely aesthetic qualities than on its originality.

(C) Museum curators would be better off not taking art critics' opinions into account when attempting to determine whether a work of art is authentic.

(D) Because it is such a skilled imitation of Vermeer, *The Disciples at Emmaus* is as artistically successful as are original paintings by artists who are less significant than Vermeer.

(E) Works of art that have little or no aesthetic value can still be said to be great achievements in artistic terms.

9. In the first paragraph, the author refers to a highly reputed critic's persistence in believing van Meegeren's forgery to be a genuine Vermeer primarily in order to

(A) argue that many art critics are inflexible in their judgments

(B) indicate that the critics who initially praised *The Disciples at Emmaus* were not as knowledgeable as they appeared

(C) suggest that the painting may yet turn out to be a genuine Vermeer

(D) emphasize that the concept of forgery itself is internally incoherent

(E) illustrate the difficulties that skillfully executed forgeries can pose for art critics

GO ON TO THE NEXT PAGE.

10. The reaction described in which one of the following scenarios is most analogous to the reaction of the art critics mentioned in line 13?

(A) lovers of a musical group contemptuously reject a tribute album recorded by various other musicians as a second-rate imitation

(B) art historians extol the work of a little-known painter as innovative until it is discovered that the painter lived much more recently than was originally thought

(C) diners at a famous restaurant effusively praise the food as delicious until they learn that the master chef is away for the night

(D) literary critics enthusiastically applaud a new novel until its author reveals that its central symbols are intended to represent political views that the critics dislike

(E) movie fans evaluate a particular movie more favorably than they otherwise might because their favorite actor plays the lead role

11. The passage provides the strongest support for inferring that Lessing holds which one of the following views?

(A) It is probable that many paintings currently hanging in important museums are actually forgeries.

(B) The historical circumstances surrounding the creation of a work are important in assessing the artistic value of that work.

(C) The greatness of an innovative artist depends on how much influence he or she has on other artists.

(D) The standards according to which a work is judged to be a forgery tend to vary from one historical period to another.

(E) An artist who makes use of techniques developed by others cannot be said to be innovative.

12. The passage most strongly supports which one of the following statements?

(A) In any historical period, the criteria by which a work is classified as a forgery can be a matter of considerable debate.

(B) An artist who uses techniques that others have developed is most likely a forger.

(C) A successful forger must originate a new artistic vision.

(D) Works of art created early in the career of a great artist are more likely than those created later to embody historic innovations.

(E) A painting can be a forgery even if it is not a copy of a particular original work of art.

13. Which one of the following, if true, would most strengthen Lessing's contention that a painting can display aesthetic excellence without possessing an equally high degree of artistic value?

(A) Many of the most accomplished art forgers have had moderately successful careers as painters of original works.

(B) Reproductions painted by talented young artists whose traditional training consisted in the copying of masterpieces were often seen as beautiful, but never regarded as great art.

(C) While experts can detect most forgeries, they can be duped by a talented forger who knows exactly what characteristics experts expect to find in the work of a particular painter.

(D) Most attempts at art forgery are ultimately unsuccessful because the forger has not mastered the necessary techniques.

(E) The criteria by which aesthetic excellence is judged change significantly from one century to another and from one culture to another.

GO ON TO THE NEXT PAGE.

Passage A

One function of language is to influence others' behavior by changing what they know, believe, or desire. For humans engaged in conversation, the perception of another's mental state is perhaps the
(5) most common vocalization stimulus.

While animal vocalizations may have evolved because they can potentially alter listeners' behavior to the signaler's benefit, such communication is—in contrast to human language—inadvertent, because
(10) most animals, with the possible exception of chimpanzees, cannot attribute mental states to others. The male *Physalaemus* frog calls because calling causes females to approach and other males to retreat, but there is no evidence that he does so because he attributes knowledge
(15) or desire to other frogs, or because he knows his calls will affect their knowledge and that this knowledge will, in turn, affect their behavior. Research also suggests that, in marked contrast to humans, nonhuman primates do not produce vocalizations in response to perception
(20) of another's need for information. Macaques, for example, give alarm calls when predators approach and coo calls upon finding food, yet experiments reveal no evidence that individuals were more likely to call about these events when they were aware of them but their offspring
(25) were clearly ignorant; similarly, chimpanzees do not appear to adjust their calling to inform ignorant individuals of their own location or that of food. Many animal vocalizations whose production initially seems goal-directed are not as purposeful as they first appear.

Passage B

(30) Many scientists distinguish animal communication systems from human language on the grounds that the former are rigid responses to stimuli, whereas human language is spontaneous and creative.

In this connection, it is commonly stated that no
(35) animal can use its communication system to lie. Obviously, a lie requires intention to deceive: to judge whether a particular instance of animal communication is truly prevarication requires knowledge of the animal's intentions. Language philosopher H. P. Grice explains
(40) that for an individual to mean something by uttering x, the individual must intend, in expressing x, to induce an audience to believe something and must also intend the utterance to be recognized as so intended. But conscious intention is a category of mental experience
(45) widely believed to be uniquely human. Philosopher Jacques Maritain's discussion of the honeybee's elaborate "waggle-dance" exemplifies this view. Although bees returning to the hive communicate to other bees the distance and direction of food sources,
(50) such communication is, Maritain asserts, merely a conditioned reflex: animals may use communicative signs but lack conscious intention regarding their use.

But these arguments are circular: conscious intention is ruled out a priori and then its absence
(55) taken as evidence that animal communication is fundamentally different from human language. In fact, the narrowing of the perceived gap between animal communication and human language revealed by recent research with chimpanzees and other animals
(60) calls into question not only the assumption that the difference between animal and human communication is qualitative rather than merely quantitative, but also the accompanying assumption that animals respond mechanically to stimuli, whereas humans speak with
(65) conscious understanding and intent.

14. Both passages are primarily concerned with addressing which one of the following questions?

(A) Are animals capable of deliberately prevaricating in order to achieve specific goals?

(B) Are the communications of animals characterized by conscious intention?

(C) What kinds of stimuli are most likely to elicit animal vocalizations?

(D) Are the communication systems of nonhuman primates qualitatively different from those of all other animals?

(E) Is there a scientific consensus about the differences between animal communication systems and human language?

15. In discussing the philosopher Maritain, the author of passage B seeks primarily to

(A) describe an interpretation of animal communication that the author believes rests on a logical error

(B) suggest by illustration that there is conscious intention underlying the communicative signs employed by certain animals

(C) present an argument in support of the view that animal communication systems are spontaneous and creative

(D) furnish specific evidence against the theory that most animal communication is merely a conditioned reflex

(E) point to a noted authority on animal communication whose views the author regards with respect

GO ON TO THE NEXT PAGE.

16. The author of passage B would be most likely to agree with which one of the following statements regarding researchers who subscribe to the position articulated in passage A?

(A) They fail to recognize that humans often communicate without any clear idea of their listeners' mental states.

(B) Most of them lack the credentials needed to assess the relevant experimental evidence correctly.

(C) They ignore well-known evidence that animals do in fact practice deception.

(D) They make assumptions about matters that should be determined empirically.

(E) They falsely believe that all communication systems can be explained in terms of their evolutionary benefits.

17. Which one of the following assertions from passage A provides support for the view attributed to Maritain in passage B (lines 50–52)?

(A) One function of language is to influence the behavior of others by changing what they think.

(B) Animal vocalizations may have evolved because they have the potential to alter listeners' behavior to the signaler's benefit.

(C) It is possible that chimpanzees may have the capacity to attribute mental states to others.

(D) There is no evidence that the male *Physalaemus* frog calls because he knows that his calls will affect the knowledge of other frogs.

(E) Macaques give alarm calls when predators approach and coo calls upon finding food.

18. The authors would be most likely to disagree over

(A) the extent to which communication among humans involves the ability to perceive the mental states of others

(B) the importance of determining to what extent animal communication systems differ from human language

(C) whether human language and animal communication differ from one another qualitatively or merely in a matter of degree

(D) whether chimpanzees' vocalizations suggest that they may possess the capacity to attribute mental states to others

(E) whether animals' vocalizations evolved to alter the behavior of other animals in a way that benefits the signaler

19. Passage B differs from passage A in that passage B is more

(A) optimistic regarding the ability of science to answer certain fundamental questions

(B) disapproving of the approach taken by others writing on the same general topic

(C) open-minded in its willingness to accept the validity of apparently conflicting positions

(D) supportive of ongoing research related to the question at hand

(E) circumspect in its refusal to commit itself to any positions with respect to still-unsettled research questions

GO ON TO THE NEXT PAGE.

In contrast to the mainstream of U.S. historiography during the late nineteenth and early twentieth centuries, African American historians of the period, such as George Washington Williams and
(5) W. E. B. DuBois, adopted a transnational perspective. This was true for several reasons, not the least of which was the necessity of doing so if certain aspects of the history of African Americans in the United States were to be treated honestly.
(10) First, there was the problem of citizenship. Even after the adoption in 1868 of the Fourteenth Amendment to the U.S. Constitution, which defined citizenship, the question of citizenship for African Americans had not been genuinely resolved. Because
(15) of this, emigrationist sentiment was a central issue in black political discourse, and both issues were critical topics for investigation. The implications for historical scholarship and national identity were enormous. While some black leaders insisted on their right to U.S.
(20) citizenship, others called on black people to emigrate and find a homeland of their own. Most African Americans were certainly not willing to relinquish their claims to the benefits of U.S. citizenship, but many had reached a point of profound pessimism and had
(25) begun to question their allegiance to the United States.
Mainstream U.S. historiography was firmly rooted in a nationalist approach during this period; the glorification of the nation and a focus on the nation-state as a historical force were dominant. The
(30) expanding spheres of influence of Europe and the United States prompted the creation of new genealogies of nations, new myths about the inevitability of nations, their "temperaments," their destinies. African American intellectuals who
(35) confronted the nationalist approach to historiography were troubled by its implications. Some argued that imperialism was a natural outgrowth of nationalism and its view that a state's strength is measured by the extension of its political power over colonial territory;
(40) the scramble for colonial empires was a distinct aspect of nationalism in the latter part of the nineteenth century.
Yet, for all their distrust of U.S. nationalism, most early black historians were themselves engaged in a
(45) sort of nation building. Deliberately or not, they contributed to the formation of a collective identity, reconstructing a glorious African past for the purposes of overturning degrading representations of blackness and establishing a firm cultural basis for a
(50) shared identity. Thus, one might argue that black historians' internationalism was a manifestation of a kind of nationalism that posits a diasporic community, which, while lacking a sovereign territory or official language, possesses a single culture, however
(55) mythical, with singular historical roots. Many members of this diaspora saw themselves as an oppressed "nation" without a homeland, or they imagined Africa as home. Hence, these historians understood their task to be the writing of the history
(60) of a people scattered by force and circumstance, a history that began in Africa.

20. Which one of the following most accurately expresses the main idea of the passage?

(A) Historians are now recognizing that the major challenge faced by African Americans in the late nineteenth and early twentieth centuries was the struggle for citizenship.

(B) Early African American historians who practiced a transnational approach to history were primarily interested in advancing an emigrationist project.

(C) U.S. historiography in the late nineteenth and early twentieth centuries was characterized by a conflict between African American historians who viewed history from a transnational perspective and mainstream historians who took a nationalist perspective.

(D) The transnational perspective of early African American historians countered mainstream nationalist historiography, but it was arguably nationalist itself to the extent that it posited a culturally unified diasporic community.

(E) Mainstream U.S. historians in the late nineteenth and early twentieth centuries could no longer justify their nationalist approach to history once they were confronted with the transnational perspective taken by African American historians.

21. Which one of the following phrases most accurately conveys the sense of the word "reconstructing" as it is used in line 47?

(A) correcting a misconception about
(B) determining the sequence of events in
(C) investigating the implications of
(D) rewarding the promoters of
(E) shaping a conception of

22. Which one of the following is most strongly supported by the passage?

(A) Emigrationist sentiment would not have been as strong among African Americans in the late nineteenth century had the promise of U.S. citizenship been fully realized for African Americans at that time.

(B) Scholars writing the history of diasporic communities generally do not discuss the forces that initially caused the scattering of the members of those communities.

(C) Most historians of the late nineteenth and early twentieth centuries endeavored to make the histories of the nations about which they wrote seem more glorious than they actually were.

(D) To be properly considered nationalist, a historical work must ignore the ways in which one nation's foreign policy decisions affected other nations.

(E) A considerable number of early African American historians embraced nationalism and the inevitability of the dominance of the nation-state.

GO ON TO THE NEXT PAGE.

23. As it is described in the passage, the transnational approach employed by African American historians working in the late nineteenth and early twentieth centuries would be best exemplified by a historical study that

(A) investigated the extent to which European and U.S. nationalist mythologies contradicted one another

(B) defined the national characters of the United States and several European nations by focusing on their treatment of minority populations rather than on their territorial ambitions

(C) recounted the attempts by the United States to gain control over new territories during the late nineteenth and early twentieth centuries

(D) considered the impact of emigrationist sentiment among African Americans on U.S. foreign policy in Africa during the late nineteenth century

(E) examined the extent to which African American culture at the turn of the century incorporated traditions that were common to a number of African cultures

24. The passage provides information sufficient to answer which one of the following questions?

(A) Which African nations did early African American historians research in writing their histories of the African diaspora?

(B) What were some of the African languages spoken by the ancestors of the members of the African diasporic community who were living in the United States in the late nineteenth century?

(C) Over which territories abroad did the United States attempt to extend its political power in the latter part of the nineteenth century?

(D) Are there textual ambiguities in the Fourteenth Amendment that spurred the conflict over U.S. citizenship for African Americans?

(E) In what ways did African American leaders respond to the question of citizenship for African Americans in the latter part of the nineteenth century?

25. The author of the passage would be most likely to agree with which one of the following statements?

(A) Members of a particular diasporic community have a common country of origin.

(B) Territorial sovereignty is not a prerequisite for the project of nation building.

(C) Early African American historians who rejected nationalist historiography declined to engage in historical myth-making of any kind.

(D) The most prominent African American historians in the late nineteenth and early twentieth centuries advocated emigration for African Americans.

(E) Historians who employed a nationalist approach focused on entirely different events from those studied and written about by early African American historians.

26. The main purpose of the second paragraph of the passage is to

(A) explain why early African American historians felt compelled to approach historiography in the way that they did

(B) show that governmental actions such as constitutional amendments do not always have the desired effect

(C) support the contention that African American intellectuals in the late nineteenth century were critical of U.S. imperialism

(D) establish that some African American political leaders in the late nineteenth century advocated emigration as an alternative to fighting for the benefits of U.S. citizenship

(E) argue that the definition of citizenship contained in the Fourteenth Amendment to the U.S. Constitution is too limited

27. As it is presented in the passage, the approach to history taken by mainstream U.S. historians of the late nineteenth and early twentieth centuries is most similar to the approach exemplified in which one of the following?

(A) An elected official writes a memo suggesting that because a particular course of action has been successful in the past, the government should continue to pursue that course of action.

(B) A biographer of a famous novelist argues that the precocity apparent in certain of the novelist's early achievements confirms that her success was attributable to innate talent.

(C) A doctor maintains that because a certain medication was developed expressly for the treatment of an illness, it is the best treatment for that illness.

(D) A newspaper runs a series of articles in order to inform the public about the environmentally hazardous practices of a large corporation.

(E) A scientist gets the same result from an experiment several times and therefore concludes that its chemical reactions always proceed in the observed fashion.

S T O P

IF YOU FINISH BEFORE TIME IS CALLED, YOU MAY CHECK YOUR WORK ON THIS SECTION ONLY.
DO NOT WORK ON ANY OTHER SECTION IN THE TEST.

SECTION II

Time—35 minutes

25 Questions

Directions: The questions in this section are based on the reasoning contained in brief statements or passages. For some questions, more than one of the choices could conceivably answer the question. However, you are to choose the best answer; that is, the response that most accurately and completely answers the question. You should not make assumptions that are by commonsense standards implausible, superfluous, or incompatible with the passage. After you have chosen the best answer, blacken the corresponding space on your answer sheet.

1. Mary to Jamal: You acknowledge that as the legitimate owner of this business I have the legal right to sell it whenever I wish. But also you claim that because loyal employees will suffer if I sell it, I therefore have no right to do so. Obviously, your statements taken together are absurd.

Mary's reasoning is most vulnerable to the criticism that she

(A) overlooks the possibility that when Jamal claims that she has no right to sell the business, he simply means she has no right to do so at this time

(B) overlooks the possibility that her employees also have rights related to the sale of the business

(C) provides no evidence for the claim that she does have a right to sell the business

(D) overlooks the possibility that Jamal is referring to two different kinds of right

(E) attacks Jamal's character rather than his argument

2. Since there is no survival value in an animal's having an organ that is able to function when all its other organs have broken down to such a degree that the animal dies, it is a result of the efficiency of natural selection that no organ is likely to evolve in such a way that it greatly outlasts the body's other organs.

Of the following, which one illustrates a principle that is most similar to the principle illustrated by the passage?

(A) A store in a lower-income neighborhood finds that it is unable to sell its higher-priced goods and so stocks them only when ordered by a customer.

(B) The body of an animal with a deficient organ is often able to compensate for that deficiency when other organs perform the task the deficient one normally performs.

(C) One car model produced by an automobile manufacturer has a life expectancy that is so much longer than its other models that its great popularity requires the manufacturer to stop producing some of the other models.

(D) Athletes occasionally overdevelop some parts of their bodies to such a great extent that other parts of their bodies are more prone to injury as a result.

(E) Automotive engineers find that it is not cost-effective to manufacture a given automobile part of such high quality that it outlasts all other parts of the automobile, as doing so would not raise the overall quality of the automobile.

GO ON TO THE NEXT PAGE.

3. Commentator: If a political administration is both economically successful and successful at protecting individual liberties, then it is an overall success. Even an administration that fails to care for the environment may succeed overall if it protects individual liberties. So far, the present administration has not cared for the environment but has successfully protected individual liberties.

If all of the statements above are true, then which one of the following must be true?

(A) The present administration is economically successful.

(B) The present administration is not an overall success.

(C) If the present administration is economically successful, then it is an overall success.

(D) If the present administration had been economically successful, it would have cared for the environment.

(E) If the present administration succeeds at environmental protection, then it will be an overall success.

4. The legislature is considering a proposed bill that would prohibit fishing in Eagle Bay. Despite widespread concern over the economic effect this ban would have on the local fishing industry, the bill should be enacted. The bay has one of the highest water pollution levels in the nation, and a recent study of the bay's fish found that 80 percent of them contained toxin levels that exceed governmental safety standards. Continuing to permit fishing in Eagle Bay could thus have grave effects on public health.

The argument proceeds by presenting evidence that

(A) the toxic contamination of fish in Eagle Bay has had grave economic effects on the local fishing industry

(B) the moral principle that an action must be judged on the basis of its foreseeable effects is usually correct

(C) the opponents of the ban have failed to weigh properly its foreseeable negative effects against its positive ones

(D) failure to enact the ban would carry with it unacceptable risks for the public welfare

(E) the ban would reduce the level of toxins in the fish in Eagle Bay

5. Vandenburg: This art museum is not adhering to its purpose. Its founders intended it to devote as much attention to contemporary art as to the art of earlier periods, but its collection of contemporary art is far smaller than its other collections.

Simpson: The relatively small size of the museum's contemporary art collection is appropriate. It's an art museum, not an ethnographic museum designed to collect every style of every period. Its contemporary art collection is small because its curators believe that there is little high-quality contemporary art.

Which one of the following principles, if valid, most helps to justify the reasoning in Simpson's response to Vandenburg?

(A) An art museum should collect only works that its curators consider to be of high artistic quality.

(B) An art museum should not collect any works that violate the purpose defined by the museum's founders.

(C) An art museum's purpose need not be to collect every style of every period.

(D) An ethnographic museum's purpose should be defined according to its curators' beliefs.

(E) The intentions of an art museum's curators should not determine what is collected by that museum.

6. Over the last five years, every new major alternative-energy initiative that initially was promised government funding has since seen that funding severely curtailed. In no such case has the government come even close to providing the level of funds initially earmarked for these projects. Since large corporations have made it a point to discourage alternative-energy projects, it is likely that the corporations' actions influenced the government's funding decisions.

Which one of the following, if true, most strengthens the reasoning above?

(A) For the past two decades, most alternative-energy initiatives have received little or no government funding.

(B) The funding initially earmarked for a government project is always subject to change, given the mechanisms by which the political process operates.

(C) The only research projects whose government funding has been severely curtailed are those that large corporations have made it a point to discourage.

(D) Some projects encouraged by large corporations have seen their funding severely curtailed over the last five years.

(E) All large corporations have made it a point to discourage some forms of research.

GO ON TO THE NEXT PAGE.

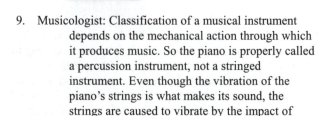

7. Talbert: Chess is beneficial for school-age children. It is enjoyable, encourages foresight and logical thinking, and discourages carelessness, inattention, and impulsiveness. In short, it promotes mental maturity.

Sklar: My objection to teaching chess to children is that it diverts mental activity from something with societal value, such as science, into something that has no societal value.

Talbert's and Sklar's statements provide the strongest support for holding that they disagree with each other over whether

(A) chess promotes mental maturity
(B) many activities promote mental maturity just as well as chess does
(C) chess is socially valuable and science is not
(D) children should be taught to play chess
(E) children who neither play chess nor study science are mentally immature

8. Marcia: Not all vegetarian diets lead to nutritional deficiencies. Research shows that vegetarians can obtain a full complement of proteins and minerals from nonanimal foods.

Theodora: You are wrong in claiming that vegetarianism cannot lead to nutritional deficiencies. If most people became vegetarians, some of those losing jobs due to the collapse of many meat-based industries would fall into poverty and hence be unable to afford a nutritionally adequate diet.

Theodora's reply to Marcia's argument is most vulnerable to criticism on the grounds that her reply

(A) is directed toward disproving a claim that Marcia did not make
(B) ignores the results of the research cited by Marcia
(C) takes for granted that no meat-based industries will collapse unless most people become vegetarians
(D) uses the word "diet" in a nontechnical sense whereas Marcia's argument uses this term in a medical sense
(E) takes for granted that people losing jobs in meat-based industries would become vegetarians

9. Musicologist: Classification of a musical instrument depends on the mechanical action through which it produces music. So the piano is properly called a percussion instrument, not a stringed instrument. Even though the vibration of the piano's strings is what makes its sound, the strings are caused to vibrate by the impact of hammers.

Which one of the following most accurately expresses the main conclusion of the musicologist's argument?

(A) Musical instruments should be classified according to the mechanical actions through which they produce sound.
(B) Musical instruments should not be classified based on the way musicians interact with them.
(C) Some people classify the piano as a stringed instrument because of the way the piano produces sound.
(D) The piano should be classified as a stringed instrument rather than as a percussion instrument.
(E) It is correct to classify the piano as a percussion instrument rather than as a stringed instrument.

10. In a vast ocean region, phosphorus levels have doubled in the past few decades due to agricultural runoff pouring out of a large river nearby. The phosphorus stimulates the growth of plankton near the ocean surface. Decaying plankton fall to the ocean floor, where bacteria devour them, consuming oxygen in the process. Due to the resulting oxygen depletion, few fish can survive in this region.

Which one of the following can be properly inferred from the information above?

(A) The agricultural runoff pouring out of the river contributes to the growth of plankton near the ocean surface.
(B) Before phosphorus levels doubled in the ocean region, most fish were able to survive in that region.
(C) If agricultural runoff ceased pouring out of the river, there would be no bacteria on the ocean floor devouring decaying plankton.
(D) The quantity of agricultural runoff pouring out of the river has doubled in the past few decades.
(E) The amount of oxygen in a body of water is in general inversely proportional to the level of phosphorus in that body of water.

GO ON TO THE NEXT PAGE.

11. Psychologists observing a shopping mall parking lot found that, on average, drivers spent 39 seconds leaving a parking space when another car was quietly waiting to enter it, 51 seconds if the driver of the waiting car honked impatiently, but only 32 seconds leaving a space when no one was waiting. This suggests that drivers feel possessive of their parking spaces even when leaving them, and that this possessiveness increases in reaction to indications that another driver wants the space.

Which one of the following, if true, most weakens the reasoning?

(A) The more pressure most drivers feel because others are waiting for them to perform maneuvers with their cars, the less quickly they are able to perform them.

(B) The amount of time drivers spend entering a parking space is not noticeably affected by whether other drivers are waiting for them to do so, nor by whether those other drivers are honking impatiently.

(C) It is considerably more difficult and time-consuming for a driver to maneuver a car out of a parking space if another car waiting to enter that space is nearby.

(D) Parking spaces in shopping mall parking lots are unrepresentative of parking spaces in general with respect to the likelihood that other cars will be waiting to enter them.

(E) Almost any driver leaving a parking space will feel angry at another driver who honks impatiently, and this anger will influence the amount of time spent leaving the space.

12. Shark teeth are among the most common vertebrate fossils; yet fossilized shark skeletons are much less common—indeed, comparatively rare among fossilized vertebrate skeletons.

Which one of the following, if true, most helps to resolve the apparent paradox described above?

(A) Unlike the bony skeletons of other vertebrates, shark skeletons are composed of cartilage, and teeth and bone are much more likely to fossilize than cartilage is.

(B) The rare fossilized skeletons of sharks that are found are often found in areas other than those in which fossils of shark teeth are plentiful.

(C) Fossils of sharks' teeth are quite difficult to distinguish from fossils of other kinds of teeth.

(D) Some species of sharks alive today grow and lose many sets of teeth during their lifetimes.

(E) The physical and chemical processes involved in the fossilization of sharks' teeth are as common as those involved in the fossilization of shark skeletons.

13. Critic: Photographers, by deciding which subjects to depict and how to depict them, express their own worldviews in their photographs, however realistically those photographs may represent reality. Thus, photographs are interpretations of reality.

The argument's conclusion is properly drawn if which one of the following is assumed?

(A) Even representing a subject realistically can involve interpreting that subject.

(B) To express a worldview is to interpret reality.

(C) All visual art expresses the artist's worldview.

(D) Any interpretation of reality involves the expression of a worldview.

(E) Nonrealistic photographs, like realistic photographs, express the worldviews of the photographers who take them.

14. Geologists recently discovered marks that closely resemble worm tracks in a piece of sandstone. These marks were made more than half a billion years earlier than the earliest known traces of multicellular animal life. Therefore, the marks are probably the traces of geological processes rather than of worms.

Which one of the following, if true, most weakens the argument?

(A) It is sometimes difficult to estimate the precise age of a piece of sandstone.

(B) Geological processes left a substantial variety of marks in sandstone more than half a billion years before the earliest known multicellular animal life existed.

(C) There were some early life forms other than worms that are known to have left marks that are hard to distinguish from those found in the piece of sandstone.

(D) At the place where the sandstone was found, the only geological processes that are likely to mark sandstone in ways that resemble worm tracks could not have occurred at the time the marks were made.

(E) Most scientists knowledgeable about early animal life believe that worms are likely to have been among the earliest forms of multicellular animal life on Earth, but evidence of their earliest existence is scarce because they are composed solely of soft tissue.

GO ON TO THE NEXT PAGE.

15. Often a type of organ or body structure is the only physically feasible means of accomplishing a given task, so it should be unsurprising if, like eyes or wings, that type of organ or body structure evolves at different times in a number of completely unrelated species. After all, whatever the difference of heritage and habitat, as organisms animals have fundamentally similar needs and so _____.

Which one of the following most logically completes the last sentence of the passage?

(A) will often live in the same environment as other species quite different from themselves

(B) will in many instances evolve similar adaptations enabling them to satisfy these needs

(C) will develop adaptations allowing them to satisfy these needs

(D) will resemble other species having different biological needs

(E) will all develop eyes or wings as adaptations

16. Engineer: Thermophotovoltaic generators are devices that convert heat into electricity. The process of manufacturing steel produces huge amounts of heat that currently go to waste. So if steel-manufacturing plants could feed the heat they produce into thermophotovoltaic generators, they would greatly reduce their electric bills, thereby saving money.

Which one of the following is an assumption on which the engineer's argument depends?

(A) There is no other means of utilizing the heat produced by the steel-manufacturing process that would be more cost effective than installing thermophotovoltaic generators.

(B) Using current technology, it would be possible for steel-manufacturing plants to feed the heat they produce into thermophotovoltaic generators in such a way that those generators could convert at least some of that heat into electricity.

(C) The amount steel-manufacturing plants would save on their electric bills by feeding heat into thermophotovoltaic generators would be sufficient to cover the cost of purchasing and installing those generators.

(D) At least some steel-manufacturing plants rely on electricity as their primary source of energy in the steel-manufacturing process.

(E) There are at least some steel-manufacturing plants that could greatly reduce their electricity bills only if they used some method of converting wasted heat or other energy from the steel-manufacturing process into electricity.

17. Herbalist: While standard antibiotics typically have just one active ingredient, herbal antibacterial remedies typically contain several. Thus, such herbal remedies are more likely to retain their effectiveness against new, resistant strains of bacteria than are standard antibiotics. For a strain of bacteria, the difficulty of developing resistance to an herbal antibacterial remedy is like a cook's difficulty in trying to prepare a single meal that will please all of several dozen guests, a task far more difficult than preparing one meal that will please a single guest.

In the analogy drawn in the argument above, which one of the following corresponds to a standard antibiotic?

(A) a single guest

(B) several dozen guests

(C) the pleasure experienced by a single guest

(D) a cook

(E) the ingredients available to a cook

18. To find out how barn owls learn how to determine the direction from which sounds originate, scientists put distorting lenses over the eyes of young barn owls before the owls first opened their eyes. The owls with these lenses behaved as if objects making sounds were farther to the right than they actually were. Once the owls matured, the lenses were removed, yet the owls continued to act as if they misjudged the location of the source of sounds. The scientists consequently hypothesized that once a barn owl has developed an auditory scheme for estimating the point from which sounds originate, it ceases to use vision to locate sounds.

The scientists' reasoning is vulnerable to which one of the following criticisms?

(A) It fails to consider whether the owls' vision was permanently impaired by their having worn the lenses while immature.

(B) It assumes that the sense of sight is equally good in all owls.

(C) It attributes human reasoning processes to a nonhuman organism.

(D) It neglects to consider how similar distorting lenses might affect the behavior of other bird species.

(E) It uses as evidence experimental results that were irrelevant to the conclusion.

GO ON TO THE NEXT PAGE.

19. As often now as in the past, newspaper journalists use direct or indirect quotation to report unsupported or false claims made by newsmakers. However, journalists are becoming less likely to openly challenge the veracity of such claims within their articles.

Each of the following, if true, helps to explain the trend in journalism described above EXCEPT:

(A) Newspaper publishers have found that many readers will cancel a subscription simply because a view they take for granted has been disputed by the publication.

(B) The areas of knowledge on which journalists report are growing in specialization and diversity, while journalists themselves are not becoming more broadly knowledgeable.

(C) Persons supporting controversial views more and more frequently choose to speak only to reporters who seem sympathetic to their views.

(D) A basic principle of journalism holds that debate over controversial issues draws the attention of the public.

(E) Journalists who challenge the veracity of claims are often criticized for failing their professional obligation to be objective.

20. When people show signs of having a heart attack an electrocardiograph (EKG) is often used to diagnose their condition. In a study, a computer program for EKG diagnosis of heart attacks was pitted against a very experienced, highly skilled cardiologist. The program correctly diagnosed a significantly higher proportion of the cases that were later confirmed to be heart attacks than did the cardiologist. Interpreting EKG data, therefore, should be left to computer programs.

Which one of the following, if true, most weakens the argument?

(A) Experts agreed that the cardiologist made few obvious mistakes in reading and interpreting the EKG data.

(B) The practice of medicine is as much an art as a science, and computer programs are not easily adapted to making subjective judgments.

(C) The cardiologist correctly diagnosed a significantly higher proportion of the cases in which no heart attack occurred than did the computer program.

(D) In a considerable percentage of cases, EKG data alone are insufficient to enable either computer programs or cardiologists to make accurate diagnoses.

(E) The cardiologist in the study was unrepresentative of cardiologists in general with respect to skill and experience.

21. A government study indicates that raising speed limits to reflect the actual average speeds of traffic on level, straight stretches of high-speed roadways reduces the accident rate. Since the actual average speed for level, straight stretches of high-speed roadways tends to be 120 kilometers per hour (75 miles per hour), that should be set as a uniform national speed limit for level, straight stretches of all such roadways.

Which one of the following principles, if valid, most helps to justify the reasoning above?

(A) Uniform national speed limits should apply only to high-speed roadways.

(B) Traffic laws applying to high-speed roadways should apply uniformly across the nation.

(C) A uniform national speed limit for high-speed roadways should be set only if all such roadways have roughly equal average speeds of traffic.

(D) Long-standing laws that are widely violated are probably not good laws.

(E) Any measure that reduces the rate of traffic accidents should be implemented.

GO ON TO THE NEXT PAGE.

22. Psychiatrist: In treating first-year students at this university, I have noticed that those reporting the highest levels of spending on recreation score at about the same level on standard screening instruments for anxiety and depression as those reporting the lowest levels of spending on recreation. This suggests that the first-year students with high levels of spending on recreation could reduce that spending without increasing their anxiety or depression.

Each of the following, if true, strengthens the psychiatrist's argument EXCEPT:

(A) At other universities, first-year students reporting the highest levels of spending on recreation also show the same degree of anxiety and depression as do those reporting the lowest levels of such spending.

(B) Screening of first-year students at the university who report moderate levels of spending on recreation reveals that those students are less anxious and depressed than both those with the highest and those with the lowest levels of spending on recreation.

(C) Among adults between the ages of 40 and 60, increased levels of spending on recreation are strongly correlated with decreased levels of anxiety and depression.

(D) The screening instruments used by the psychiatrist are extremely accurate in revealing levels of anxiety and depression among university students.

(E) Several of the psychiatrist's patients who are first-year students at the university have reduced their spending on recreation from very high levels to very low levels without increasing their anxiety or depression.

23. Every brick house on River Street has a front yard. Most of the houses on River Street that have front yards also have two stories. So most of the brick houses on River Street have two stories.

Which one of the following is most appropriate as an analogy demonstrating that the reasoning in the argument above is flawed?

(A) By that line of reasoning, we could conclude that most politicians have run for office, since all legislators are politicians and most legislators have run for office.

(B) By that line of reasoning, we could conclude that most public servants are legislators, since most legislators have run for office and most politicians who have run for office are public servants.

(C) By that line of reasoning, we could conclude that not every public servant has run for office, since every legislator is a public servant but some public servants are not legislators.

(D) By that line of reasoning, we could conclude that most legislators have never run for office, since most public servants have never run for office and all legislators are public servants.

(E) By that line of reasoning, we could conclude that most legislators are not public servants, since most public servants have not run for office and most legislators have run for office.

GO ON TO THE NEXT PAGE.

24. Historian: It is unlikely that someone would see history
as the working out of moral themes unless he or
she held clear and unambiguous moral beliefs.
However, one's inclination to morally judge
human behavior decreases as one's knowledge of
history increases. Consequently, the more history
a person knows, the less likely that person is to
view history as the working out of moral themes.

The conclusion of the argument is properly drawn if
which one of the following is assumed?

(A)   Historical events that fail to elicit moral
disapproval are generally not considered to
exemplify a moral theme.
(B)   The less inclined one is to morally judge human
behavior, the less likely it is that one holds
clear and unambiguous moral beliefs.
(C)   Only those who do not understand human
history attribute moral significance to historical
events.
(D)   The more clear and unambiguous one's moral
beliefs, the more likely one is to view history
as the working out of moral themes.
(E)   People tend to be less objective regarding a
subject about which they possess extensive
knowledge than regarding a subject about
which they do not possess extensive
knowledge.

25. A recent poll revealed that most students at our
university prefer that the university, which is searching
for a new president, hire someone who has extensive
experience as a university president. However, in the
very same poll, the person most students chose from
among a list of leading candidates as the one they
would most like to see hired was someone who has
never served as a university president.

Which one of the following, if true, most helps to
account for the apparent discrepancy in the students'
preferences?

(A)   Because several of the candidates listed in the
poll had extensive experience as university
presidents, not all of the candidates could be
differentiated on this basis alone.
(B)   Most of the candidates listed in the poll had
extensive experience as university presidents.
(C)   Students taking the poll had fewer candidates to
choose from than were currently being
considered for the position.
(D)   Most of the students taking the poll did not
know whether any of the leading candidates
listed in the poll had ever served as a
university president.
(E)   Often a person can be well suited to a position
even though they have relatively little
experience in such a position.

S T O P

IF YOU FINISH BEFORE TIME IS CALLED, YOU MAY CHECK YOUR WORK ON THIS SECTION ONLY.
DO NOT WORK ON ANY OTHER SECTION IN THE TEST.

SECTION III
Time—35 minutes
23 Questions

Directions: Each group of questions in this section is based on a set of conditions. In answering some of the questions, it may be useful to draw a rough diagram. Choose the response that most accurately and completely answers each question and blacken the corresponding space on your answer sheet.

Questions 1–5

Exactly six workers—Faith, Gus, Hannah, Juan, Kenneth, and Lisa—will travel to a business convention in two cars—car 1 and car 2. Each car must carry at least two of the workers, one of whom will be assigned to drive. For the entire trip, the workers will comply with an assignment that also meets the following constraints:

Either Faith or Gus must drive the car in which Hannah travels.
Either Faith or Kenneth must drive the car in which Juan travels.
Gus must travel in the same car as Lisa.

1. Which one of the following is a possible assignment of the workers to the cars?

   (A) car 1: Faith (driver), Hannah, and Juan
       car 2: Gus (driver), Kenneth, and Lisa
   (B) car 1: Faith (driver), Hannah, and Kenneth
       car 2: Lisa (driver), Gus, and Juan
   (C) car 1: Faith (driver), Juan, Kenneth, and Lisa
       car 2: Gus (driver) and Hannah
   (D) car 1: Faith (driver) and Juan
       car 2: Kenneth (driver), Gus, Hannah, and Lisa
   (E) car 1: Gus (driver), Hannah, and Lisa
       car 2: Juan (driver), Faith, and Kenneth

2. The two workers who drive the cars CANNOT be

   (A) Faith and Gus
   (B) Faith and Kenneth
   (C) Faith and Lisa
   (D) Gus and Kenneth
   (E) Kenneth and Lisa

3. If Lisa drives one of the cars, then which one of the following could be true?

   (A) Faith travels in the same car as Kenneth.
   (B) Faith travels in the same car as Lisa.
   (C) Gus travels in the same car as Hannah.
   (D) Gus travels in the same car as Juan.
   (E) Hannah travels in the same car as Lisa.

4. If Faith travels with two other workers in car 1, and if Faith is not the driver, then the person in car 1 other than Faith and the driver must be

   (A) Gus
   (B) Hannah
   (C) Juan
   (D) Kenneth
   (E) Lisa

5. Which one of the following CANNOT be true?

   (A) Gus is the only person other than the driver in one of the cars.
   (B) Hannah is the only person other than the driver in one of the cars.
   (C) Juan is the only person other than the driver in one of the cars.
   (D) Kenneth is the only person other than the driver in one of the cars.
   (E) Lisa is the only person other than the driver in one of the cars.

GO ON TO THE NEXT PAGE.

Questions 6–11

An archaeologist has six ancient artifacts—a figurine, a headdress, a jar, a necklace, a plaque, and a tureen—no two of which are the same age. She will order them from first (oldest) to sixth (most recent). The following has already been determined:

The figurine is older than both the jar and the headdress.
The necklace and the jar are both older than the tureen.
Either the plaque is older than both the headdress and the necklace, or both the headdress and the necklace are older than the plaque.

6. Which one of the following could be the artifacts in the order of their age, from first to sixth?

(A)   figurine, headdress, jar, necklace, plaque, tureen
(B)   figurine, jar, plaque, headdress, tureen, necklace
(C)   figurine, necklace, plaque, headdress, jar, tureen
(D)   necklace, jar, figurine, headdress, plaque, tureen
(E)   plaque, tureen, figurine, necklace, jar, headdress

7. Exactly how many of the artifacts are there any one of which could be first?

(A)   one
(B)   two
(C)   three
(D)   four
(E)   five

8. Which one of the following artifacts CANNOT be fourth?

(A)   figurine
(B)   headdress
(C)   jar
(D)   necklace
(E)   plaque

9. If the figurine is third, which one of the following must be second?

(A)   headdress
(B)   jar
(C)   necklace
(D)   plaque
(E)   tureen

10. If the plaque is first, then exactly how many artifacts are there any one of which could be second?

(A)   one
(B)   two
(C)   three
(D)   four
(E)   five

11. Which one of the following, if substituted for the information that the necklace and the jar are both older than the tureen, would have the same effect in determining the order of the artifacts?

(A)   The tureen is older than the headdress but not as old as the figurine.
(B)   The figurine and the necklace are both older than the tureen.
(C)   The necklace is older than the tureen if and only if the jar is.
(D)   All of the artifacts except the headdress and the plaque must be older than the tureen.
(E)   The plaque is older than the necklace if and only if the plaque is older than the tureen.

GO ON TO THE NEXT PAGE.

Questions 12–17

The coach of a women's track team must determine which four of five runners—Quinn, Ramirez, Smith, Terrell, and Uzoma—will run in the four races of an upcoming track meet. Each of the four runners chosen will run in exactly one of the four races—the first, second, third, or fourth. The coach's selection is bound by the following constraints:

If Quinn runs in the track meet, then Terrell runs in the race immediately after the race in which Quinn runs.

Smith does not run in either the second race or the fourth race.

If Uzoma does not run in the track meet, then Ramirez runs in the second race.

If Ramirez runs in the second race, then Uzoma does not run in the track meet.

12. Which one of the following could be the order in which the runners run, from first to fourth?

(A) Uzoma, Ramirez, Quinn, Terrell
(B) Terrell, Smith, Ramirez, Uzoma
(C) Smith, Ramirez, Terrell, Quinn
(D) Ramirez, Uzoma, Smith, Terrell
(E) Quinn, Terrell, Smith, Ramirez

13. Which one of the following runners must the coach select to run in the track meet?

(A) Quinn
(B) Ramirez
(C) Smith
(D) Terrell
(E) Uzoma

14. The question of which runners will be chosen to run in the track meet and in what races they will run can be completely resolved if which one of the following is true?

(A) Ramirez runs in the first race.
(B) Ramirez runs in the second race.
(C) Ramirez runs in the third race.
(D) Ramirez runs in the fourth race.
(E) Ramirez does not run in the track meet.

15. Which one of the following CANNOT be true?

(A) Ramirez runs in the race immediately before the race in which Smith runs.
(B) Smith runs in the race immediately before the race in which Quinn runs.
(C) Smith runs in the race immediately before the race in which Terrell runs.
(D) Terrell runs in the race immediately before the race in which Ramirez runs.
(E) Uzoma runs in the race immediately before the race in which Terrell runs.

16. If Uzoma runs in the first race, then which one of the following must be true?

(A) Quinn does not run in the track meet.
(B) Smith does not run in the track meet.
(C) Quinn runs in the second race.
(D) Terrell runs in the second race.
(E) Ramirez runs in the fourth race.

17. If both Quinn and Smith run in the track meet, then how many of the runners are there any one of whom could be the one who runs in the first race?

(A) one
(B) two
(C) three
(D) four
(E) five

GO ON TO THE NEXT PAGE.

Questions 18–23

From the 1st through the 7th of next month, seven nurses—Farnham, Griseldi, Heany, Juarez, Khan, Lightfoot, and Moreau—will each conduct one information session at a community center. Each nurse's session will fall on a different day. The nurses' schedule is governed by the following constraints:

At least two of the other nurses' sessions must fall in between Heany's session and Moreau's session.

Griseldi's session must be on the day before Khan's.

Juarez's session must be on a later day than Moreau's.

Farnham's session must be on an earlier day than Khan's but on a later day than Lightfoot's.

Lightfoot cannot conduct the session on the 2nd.

18. Which one of the following could be the order of the nurses' sessions, from first to last?

(A) Farnham, Griseldi, Khan, Moreau, Juarez, Lightfoot, Heany
(B) Heany, Lightfoot, Farnham, Moreau, Juarez, Griseldi, Khan
(C) Juarez, Heany, Lightfoot, Farnham, Moreau, Griseldi, Khan
(D) Lightfoot, Moreau, Farnham, Juarez, Griseldi, Khan, Heany
(E) Moreau, Lightfoot, Heany, Juarez, Farnham, Griseldi, Khan

19. Juarez's session CANNOT be on which one of the following days?

(A) the 2nd
(B) the 3rd
(C) the 5th
(D) the 6th
(E) the 7th

20. If Juarez's session is on the 3rd, then which one of the following could be true?

(A) Moreau's session is on the 1st.
(B) Khan's session is on the 5th.
(C) Heany's session is on the 6th.
(D) Griseldi's session is on the 5th.
(E) Farnham's session is on the 2nd.

21. If Khan's session is on an earlier day than Moreau's, which one of the following could conduct the session on the 3rd?

(A) Griseldi
(B) Heany
(C) Juarez
(D) Lightfoot
(E) Moreau

22. If Griseldi's session is on the 5th, then which one of the following must be true?

(A) Farnham's session is on the 3rd.
(B) Heany's session is on the 7th.
(C) Juarez's session is on the 4th.
(D) Lightfoot's session is on the 1st.
(E) Moreau's session is on the 2nd.

23. Lightfoot's session could be on which one of the following days?

(A) the 3rd
(B) the 4th
(C) the 5th
(D) the 6th
(E) the 7th

S T O P

IF YOU FINISH BEFORE TIME IS CALLED, YOU MAY CHECK YOUR WORK ON THIS SECTION ONLY.
DO NOT WORK ON ANY OTHER SECTION IN THE TEST.

SECTION IV

Time—35 minutes

26 Questions

Directions: The questions in this section are based on the reasoning contained in brief statements or passages. For some questions, more than one of the choices could conceivably answer the question. However, you are to choose the best answer; that is, the response that most accurately and completely answers the question. You should not make assumptions that are by commonsense standards implausible, superfluous, or incompatible with the passage. After you have chosen the best answer, blacken the corresponding space on your answer sheet.

1. Among Trinidadian guppies, males with large spots are more attractive to females than are males with small spots, who consequently are presented with less frequent mating opportunities. Yet guppies with small spots are more likely to avoid detection by predators, so in waters where predators are abundant only guppies with small spots live to maturity.

    The situation described above most closely conforms to which one of the following generalizations?

    (A) A trait that helps attract mates is sometimes more dangerous to one sex than to another.
    (B) Those organisms that are most attractive to the opposite sex have the greatest number of offspring.
    (C) Those organisms that survive the longest have the greatest number of offspring.
    (D) Whether a trait is harmful to the organisms of a species can depend on which sex possesses it.
    (E) A trait that is helpful to procreation can also hinder it in certain environments.

2. Programmer: We computer programmers at Mytheco are demanding raises to make our average salary comparable with that of the technical writers here who receive, on average, 20 percent more in salary and benefits than we do. This pay difference is unfair and intolerable.

    Mytheco executive: But many of the technical writers have worked for Mytheco longer than have many of the programmers. Since salary and benefits at Mytheco are directly tied to seniority, the 20 percent pay difference you mention is perfectly acceptable.

    Evaluating the adequacy of the Mytheco executive's response requires a clarification of which one of the following?

    (A) whether any of the technical writers at Mytheco once worked as programmers at the company
    (B) how the average seniority of programmers compares with the average seniority of technical writers
    (C) whether the sorts of benefits an employee of Mytheco receives are tied to the salary of that employee
    (D) whether the Mytheco executive was at one time a technical writer employed by Mytheco
    (E) how the Mytheco executive's salary compares with that of the programmers

3. Cable TV stations have advantages that enable them to attract many more advertisers than broadcast networks attract. For example, cable stations are able to target particular audiences with 24-hour news, sports, or movies, whereas broadcast networks must offer a variety of programming. Cable can also offer lower advertising rates than any broadcast network can, because it is subsidized by viewers through subscriber fees. Additionally, many cable stations have expanded worldwide with multinational programming.

    The statements above, if true, provide support for each of the following EXCEPT:

    (A) Some broadcast networks can be viewed in several countries.
    (B) Broadcast networks do not rely on subscriber fees from viewers.
    (C) Low costs are often an important factor for advertisers in selecting a station or network on which to run a TV ad.
    (D) Some advertisers prefer to have the opportunity to address a worldwide audience.
    (E) The audiences that some advertisers prefer to target watch 24-hour news stations.

4. In polluted industrial English cities during the Industrial Revolution, two plant diseases—black spot, which infects roses, and tar spot, which infects sycamore trees—disappeared. It is likely that air pollution eradicated these diseases.

    Which one of the following, if true, most strengthens the reasoning above?

    (A) Scientists theorize that some plants can develop a resistance to air pollution.
    (B) Certain measures help prevent infection by black spot and tar spot, but once infection occurs, it is very difficult to eliminate.
    (C) For many plant species, scientists have not determined the effects of air pollution.
    (D) Black spot and tar spot returned when the air in the cities became less polluted.
    (E) Black spot and tar spot were the only plant diseases that disappeared in any English cities during the Industrial Revolution.

GO ON TO THE NEXT PAGE.

5. Many scholars are puzzled about who created the seventeenth-century abridgment of Shakespeare's *Hamlet* contained in the First Quarto. Two facts about the work shed light on this question. First, the person who undertook the abridgment clearly did not possess a copy of *Hamlet*. Second, the abridgment contains a very accurate rendering of the speeches of one of the characters, but a slipshod handling of all the other parts.

    Which one of the following statements is most supported by the information above?

    (A)   The abridgment was prepared by Shakespeare.
    (B)   The abridgment was created to make *Hamlet* easier to produce on stage.
    (C)   The abridgment was produced by an actor who had played a role in *Hamlet*.
    (D)   The abridgement was prepared by a spectator of a performance of *Hamlet*.
    (E)   The abridgment was produced by an actor who was trying to improve the play.

6. Musicologist: Many critics complain of the disproportion between text and music in Handel's *da capo* arias. These texts are generally quite short and often repeated well beyond what is needed for literal understanding. Yet such criticism is refuted by noting that repetition serves a vital function: it frees the audience to focus on the music itself, which can speak to audiences whatever their language.

    Which one of the following sentences best expresses the main point of the musicologist's reasoning?

    (A)   Handel's *da capo* arias contain a disproportionate amount of music.
    (B)   Handel's *da capo* arias are superior to most in their accessibility to diverse audiences.
    (C)   At least one frequent criticism of Handel's *da capo* arias is undeserved.
    (D)   At least some of Handel's *da capo* arias contain unnecessary repetitions.
    (E)   Most criticism of Handel's *da capo* arias is unwarranted.

7. Baxe Interiors, one of the largest interior design companies in existence, currently has a near monopoly in the corporate market. Several small design companies have won prestigious awards for their corporate work, while Baxe has won none. Nonetheless, the corporate managers who solicit design proposals will only contract with companies they believe are unlikely to go bankrupt, and they believe that only very large companies are unlikely to go bankrupt.

    The statements above, if true, most strongly support which one of the following?

    (A)   There are other very large design companies besides Baxe, but they produce designs that are inferior to Baxe's.
    (B)   Baxe does not have a near monopoly in the market of any category of interior design other than corporate interiors.
    (C)   For the most part, designs that are produced by small companies are superior to the designs produced by Baxe.
    (D)   At least some of the corporate managers who solicit design proposals are unaware that there are designs that are much better than those produced by Baxe.
    (E)   The existence of interior designs that are superior to those produced by Baxe does not currently threaten its near monopoly in the corporate market.

GO ON TO THE NEXT PAGE.

8. The giant Chicxulub crater in Mexico provides indisputable evidence that a huge asteroid, about six miles across, struck Earth around the time many of the last dinosaur species were becoming extinct. But this catastrophe was probably not responsible for most of these extinctions. Any major asteroid strike kills many organisms in or near the region of the impact, but there is little evidence that such a strike could have a worldwide effect. Indeed, some craters even larger than the Chicxulub crater were made during times in Earth's history when there were no known extinctions.

Which one of the following, if true, would most weaken the argument?

(A) The vast majority of dinosaur species are known to have gone extinct well before the time of the asteroid impact that produced the Chicxulub crater.

(B) The size of a crater caused by an asteroid striking Earth generally depends on both the size of that asteroid and the force of its impact.

(C) Fossils have been discovered of a number of dinosaurs that clearly died as a result of the asteroid impact that produced the Chicxulub crater.

(D) There is no evidence that any other asteroid of equal size struck Earth at the same time as the asteroid that produced the Chicxulub crater.

(E) During the period immediately before the asteroid that produced the Chicxulub crater struck, most of the world's dinosaurs lived in or near the region of the asteroid's impending impact.

9. In a sample containing 1,000 peanuts from lot A and 1,000 peanuts from lot B, 50 of the peanuts from lot A were found to be infected with *Aspergillus*. Two hundred of the peanuts from lot B were found to be infected with *Aspergillus*. Therefore, infection with *Aspergillus* is more widespread in lot B than in lot A.

The reasoning in which one of the following is most similar to the reasoning in the argument above?

(A) Every one of these varied machine parts is of uniformly high quality. Therefore, the machine that we assemble from them will be of equally high quality.

(B) If a plant is carelessly treated, it is likely to develop blight. If a plant develops blight, it is likely to die. Therefore, if a plant is carelessly treated, it is likely to die.

(C) In the past 1,000 experiments, whenever an experimental fungicide was applied to coffee plants infected with coffee rust, the infection disappeared. The coffee rust never disappeared before the fungicide was applied. Therefore, in these experiments, application of the fungicide caused the disappearance of coffee rust.

(D) Three thousand registered voters—1,500 members of the Liberal party and 1,500 members of the Conservative party—were asked which mayoral candidate they favored. Four hundred of the Liberals and 300 of the Conservatives favored Pollack. Therefore, Pollack has more support among Liberals than among Conservatives.

(E) All of my livestock are registered with the regional authority. None of the livestock registered with the regional authority are free-range livestock. Therefore, none of my livestock are free-range livestock.

GO ON TO THE NEXT PAGE.

10. Economist: If the belief were to become widespread that losing one's job is not a sign of personal shortcomings but instead an effect of impersonal social forces (which is surely correct), there would be growth in the societal demand for more government control of the economy to protect individuals from these forces, just as the government now protects them from military invasion. Such extensive government control of the economy would lead to an economic disaster, however.

The economist's statements, if true, most strongly support which one of the following?

(A) Increased knowledge of the causes of job loss could lead to economic disaster.

(B) An individual's belief in his or her own abilities is the only reliable protection against impersonal social forces.

(C) Governments should never interfere with economic forces.

(D) Societal demand for government control of the economy is growing.

(E) In general, people should feel no more responsible for economic disasters than for military invasions.

11. A development company has proposed building an airport near the city of Dalton. If the majority of Dalton's residents favor the proposal, the airport will be built. However, it is unlikely that a majority of Dalton's residents would favor the proposal, for most of them believe that the airport would create noise problems. Thus, it is unlikely that the airport will be built.

The reasoning in the argument is flawed in that the argument

(A) treats a sufficient condition for the airport's being built as a necessary condition

(B) concludes that something must be true, because most people believe it to be true

(C) concludes, on the basis that a certain event is unlikely to occur, that the event will not occur

(D) fails to consider whether people living near Dalton would favor building the airport

(E) overlooks the possibility that a new airport could benefit the local economy

12. After the rush-hour speed limit on the British M25 motorway was lowered from 70 miles per hour (115 kilometers per hour) to 50 miles per hour (80 kilometers per hour), rush-hour travel times decreased by approximately 15 percent.

Which one of the following, if true, most helps to explain the decrease in travel times described above?

(A) After the decrease in the rush-hour speed limit, the average speed on the M25 was significantly lower during rush hours than at other times of the day.

(B) Travel times during periods other than rush hours were essentially unchanged after the rush-hour speed limit was lowered.

(C) Before the rush-hour speed limit was lowered, rush-hour accidents that caused lengthy delays were common, and most of these accidents were caused by high-speed driving.

(D) Enforcement of speed limits on the M25 was quite rigorous both before and after the rush-hour speed limit was lowered.

(E) The number of people who drive on the M25 during rush hours did not increase after the rush-hour speed limit was lowered.

13. An art critic, by ridiculing an artwork, can undermine the pleasure one takes in it; conversely, by lavishing praise upon an artwork, an art critic can render the experience of viewing the artwork more pleasurable. So an artwork's artistic merit can depend not only on the person who creates it but also on those who critically evaluate it.

The conclusion can be properly drawn if which one of the following is assumed?

(A) The merit of an artistic work is determined by the amount of pleasure it elicits.

(B) Most people lack the confidence necessary for making their own evaluations of art.

(C) Art critics understand what gives an artwork artistic merit better than artists do.

(D) Most people seek out critical reviews of particular artworks before viewing those works.

(E) The pleasure people take in something is typically influenced by what they think others feel about it.

GO ON TO THE NEXT PAGE.

14. The number of automobile thefts has declined steadily during the past five years, and it is more likely now than it was five years ago that someone who steals a car will be convicted of the crime.

Which one of the following, if true, most helps to explain the facts cited above?

(A) Although there are fewer car thieves now than there were five years ago, the proportion of thieves who tend to abandon cars before their owners notice that they have been stolen has also decreased.

(B) Car alarms are more common than they were five years ago, but their propensity to be triggered in the absence of any criminal activity has resulted in people generally ignoring them when they are triggered.

(C) An upsurge in home burglaries over the last five years has required police departments to divert limited resources to investigation of these cases.

(D) Because of the increasingly lucrative market for stolen automobile parts, many stolen cars are quickly disassembled and the parts are sold to various buyers across the country.

(E) There are more adolescent car thieves now than there were five years ago, and the sentences given to young criminals tend to be far more lenient than those given to adult criminals.

15. Legislator: My staff conducted a poll in which my constituents were asked whether they favor high taxes. More than 97 percent answered "no." Clearly, then, my constituents would support the bill I recently introduced, which reduces the corporate income tax.

The reasoning in the legislator's argument is most vulnerable to criticism on the grounds that the argument

(A) fails to establish that the opinions of the legislator's constituents are representative of the opinions of the country's population as a whole

(B) fails to consider whether the legislator's constituents consider the current corporate income tax a high tax

(C) confuses an absence of evidence that the legislator's constituents oppose a bill with the existence of evidence that the legislator's constituents support that bill

(D) draws a conclusion that merely restates a claim presented in support of that conclusion

(E) treats a result that proves that the public supports a bill as a result that is merely consistent with public support for that bill

16. Many nursing homes have prohibitions against having pets, and these should be lifted. The presence of an animal companion can yield health benefits by reducing a person's stress. A pet can also make one's time at a home more rewarding, which will be important to more people as the average life span of our population increases.

Which one of the following most accurately expresses the conclusion drawn in the argument above?

(A) As the average life span increases, it will be important to more people that life in nursing homes be rewarding.

(B) Residents of nursing homes should enjoy the same rewarding aspects of life as anyone else.

(C) The policy that many nursing homes have should be changed so that residents are allowed to have pets.

(D) Having a pet can reduce one's stress and thereby make one a healthier person.

(E) The benefits older people derive from having pets need to be recognized, especially as the average life span increases.

17. Near many cities, contamination of lakes and rivers from pollutants in rainwater runoff exceeds that from industrial discharge. As the runoff washes over buildings and pavements, it picks up oil and other pollutants. Thus, water itself is among the biggest water polluters.

The statement that contamination of lakes and rivers from pollutants in rainwater runoff exceeds that from industrial discharge plays which one of the following roles in the argument?

(A) It is a conclusion for which the claim that water itself should be considered a polluter is offered as support.

(B) It is cited as evidence that pollution from rainwater runoff is a more serious problem than pollution from industrial discharge.

(C) It is a generalization based on the observation that rainwater runoff picks up oil and other pollutants as it washes over buildings and pavements.

(D) It is a premise offered in support of the conclusion that water itself is among the biggest water polluters.

(E) It is stated to provide an example of a typical kind of city pollution.

GO ON TO THE NEXT PAGE.

18. Wong: Although all countries are better off as democracies, a transitional autocratic stage is sometimes required before a country can become democratic.

    Tate: The freedom and autonomy that democracy provides are of genuine value, but the simple material needs of people are more important. Some countries can better meet these needs as autocracies than as democracies.

    Wong's and Tate's statements provide the most support for the claim that they disagree over the truth of which one of the following?

    (A)   There are some countries that are better off as autocracies than as democracies.
    (B)   Nothing is more important to a country than the freedom and autonomy of the individuals who live in that country.
    (C)   In some cases, a country cannot become a democracy.
    (D)   The freedom and autonomy that democracy provides are of genuine value.
    (E)   All democracies succeed in meeting the simple material needs of people.

19. Principle: When none of the fully qualified candidates for a new position at Arvue Corporation currently works for that company, it should hire the candidate who would be most productive in that position.

    Application: Arvue should not hire Krall for the new position, because Delacruz is a candidate and is fully qualified.

    Which one of the following, if true, justifies the above application of the principle?

    (A)   All of the candidates are fully qualified for the new position, but none already works for Arvue.
    (B)   Of all the candidates who do not already work for Arvue, Delacruz would be the most productive in the new position.
    (C)   Krall works for Arvue, but Delacruz is the candidate who would be most productive in the new position.
    (D)   Several candidates currently work for Arvue, but Krall and Delacruz do not.
    (E)   None of the candidates already works for Arvue, and Delacruz is the candidate who would be most productive in the new position.

20. Many important types of medicine have been developed from substances discovered in plants that grow only in tropical rain forests. There are thousands of plant species in these rain forests that have not yet been studied by scientists, and it is very likely that many such plants also contain substances of medicinal value. Thus, if the tropical rain forests are not preserved, important types of medicine will never be developed.

    Which one of the following is an assumption required by the argument?

    (A)   There are substances of medicinal value contained in tropical rain forest plants not yet studied by scientists that differ from those substances already discovered in tropical rain forest plants.
    (B)   Most of the tropical rain forest plants that contain substances of medicinal value can also be found growing in other types of environment.
    (C)   The majority of plant species that are unique to tropical rain forests and that have been studied by scientists have been discovered to contain substances of medicinal value.
    (D)   Any substance of medicinal value contained in plant species indigenous to tropical rain forests will eventually be discovered if those species are studied by scientists.
    (E)   The tropical rain forests should be preserved to make it possible for important medicines to be developed from plant species that have not yet been studied by scientists.

GO ON TO THE NEXT PAGE.

21. In modern deep-diving marine mammals, such as whales, the outer shell of the bones is porous. This has the effect of making the bones light enough so that it is easy for the animals to swim back to the surface after a deep dive. The outer shell of the bones was also porous in the ichthyosaur, an extinct prehistoric marine reptile. We can conclude from this that ichthyosaurs were deep divers.

Which one of the following, if true, most weakens the argument?

(A)   Some deep-diving marine species must surface after dives but do not have bones with porous outer shells.

(B)   In most modern marine reptile species, the outer shell of the bones is not porous.

(C)   In most modern and prehistoric marine reptile species that are not deep divers, the outer shell of the bones is porous.

(D)   In addition to the porous outer shells of their bones, whales have at least some characteristics suited to deep diving for which there is no clear evidence whether these were shared by ichthyosaurs.

(E)   There is evidence that the bones of ichthyosaurs would have been light enough to allow surfacing even if the outer shells were not porous.

22.   Librarian: Some argue that the preservation grant we received should be used to restore our original copy of our town's charter, since if the charter is not restored, it will soon deteriorate beyond repair. But this document, although sentimentally important, has no scholarly value. Copies are readily available. Since we are a research library and not a museum, the money would be better spent preserving documents that have significant scholarly value.

The claim that the town's charter, if not restored, will soon deteriorate beyond repair plays which one of the following roles in the librarian's argument?

(A)   It is a claim that the librarian's argument attempts to show to be false.

(B)   It is the conclusion of the argument that the librarian's argument rejects.

(C)   It is a premise in an argument whose conclusion is rejected by the librarian's argument.

(D)   It is a premise used to support the librarian's main conclusion.

(E)   It is a claim whose truth is required by the librarian's argument.

23.   Columnist: Although much has been learned, we are still largely ignorant of the intricate interrelationships among species of living organisms. We should, therefore, try to preserve the maximum number of species if we have an interest in preserving any, since allowing species toward which we are indifferent to perish might undermine the viability of other species.

Which one of the following principles, if valid, most helps to justify the columnist's argument?

(A)   It is strongly in our interest to preserve certain plant and animal species.

(B)   We should not take any action until all relevant scientific facts have been established and taken into account.

(C)   We should not allow the number of species to diminish any further than is necessary for the flourishing of present and future human populations.

(D)   We should not allow a change to occur unless we are assured that that change will not jeopardize anything that is important to us.

(E)   We should always undertake the course of action that is likely to have the best consequences in the immediate future.

24.   One is likely to feel comfortable approaching a stranger if the stranger is of one's approximate age. Therefore, long-term friends are probably of the same approximate age as each other since most long-term friendships begin because someone felt comfortable approaching a stranger.

The reasoning in the argument is flawed in that it

(A)   presumes, without warrant, that one is likely to feel uncomfortable approaching a person only if that person is a stranger

(B)   infers that a characteristic is present in a situation from the fact that that characteristic is present in most similar situations

(C)   overlooks the possibility that one is less likely to feel comfortable approaching someone who is one's approximate age if that person is a stranger than if that person is not a stranger

(D)   presumes, without warrant, that one never approaches a stranger unless one feels comfortable doing so

(E)   fails to address whether one is likely to feel comfortable approaching a stranger who is not one's approximate age

GO ON TO THE NEXT PAGE.

25. There can be no individual freedom without the rule of law, for there is no individual freedom without social integrity, and pursuing the good life is not possible without social integrity.

The conclusion drawn above follows logically if which one of the following is assumed?

(A) There can be no rule of law without social integrity.

(B) There can be no social integrity without the rule of law.

(C) One cannot pursue the good life without the rule of law.

(D) Social integrity is possible only if individual freedom prevails.

(E) There can be no rule of law without individual freedom.

26. Economist: Countries with an uneducated population are destined to be weak economically and politically, whereas those with an educated population have governments that display a serious financial commitment to public education. So any nation with a government that has made such a commitment will avoid economic and political weakness.

The pattern of flawed reasoning in which one of the following arguments is most similar to that in the economist's argument?

(A) Animal species with a very narrow diet will have more difficulty surviving if the climate suddenly changes, but a species with a broader diet will not; for changes in the climate can remove the traditional food supply.

(B) People incapable of empathy are not good candidates for public office, but those who do have the capacity for empathy are able to manipulate others easily; hence, people who can manipulate others are good candidates for public office.

(C) People who cannot give orders are those who do not understand the personalities of the people to whom they give orders. Thus, those who can give orders are those who understand the personalities of the people to whom they give orders.

(D) Poets who create poetry of high quality are those who have studied traditional poetry, because poets who have not studied traditional poetry are the poets most likely to create something shockingly inventive, and poetry that is shockingly inventive is rarely fine poetry.

(E) People who dislike exercise are unlikely to lose weight without sharply curtailing their food intake; but since those who dislike activity generally tend to avoid it, people who like to eat but dislike exercise will probably fail to lose weight.

S T O P

IF YOU FINISH BEFORE TIME IS CALLED, YOU MAY CHECK YOUR WORK ON THIS SECTION ONLY.
DO NOT WORK ON ANY OTHER SECTION IN THE TEST.

Acknowledgment is made to the following sources from which material has been adapted for use in this test booklet:

Robin D. G. Kelley, "But a Local Phase of a World Problem: Black History's Global Vision, 1883–1950." ©1999 by the Organization of American Historians.

Alfred Lessing, "What Is Wrong With a Forgery?" in The Forger's Art. ©1983 by The Regents of the University of California.

David Pitts, "The Noble Endeavor: The Creation of the Universal Declaration of Human Rights." ©2001 by U.S. Department of State, Office of International Information Programs.

Ellen Rosand, "It Bears Repeating." ©1996 by Metropolitan Opera Guild, Inc.

Topic Code	Print Your Full Name Here		
097214	Last	First	M.I.

Date	Sign Your Name Here
/ /	

LSAC®

Scratch Paper
Do not write your essay in this space.

LSAT® Writing Sample Topic

Directions: The scenario presented below describes two choices, either one of which can be supported on the basis of the information given. Your essay should consider both choices and argue for one over the other, based on the two specified criteria and the facts provided. There is no "right" or "wrong" choice: a reasonable argument can be made for either.

The attorneys for the plaintiffs in a lawsuit against a major pharmaceutical company are choosing an expert scientific witness to testify that a drug produced by the company was responsible for serious side effects. The attorneys have narrowed their choices down to two people. Using the facts below, write an essay in which you argue for choosing one person over the other based on the following two criteria:

- The attorneys want a witness who will be able to communicate technical information in a clear and effective manner to the jury.
- The attorneys want a witness who is highly knowledgeable in the field of pharmacology.

Dr. Rosa Benally has qualifications similar to those of the defense team's expert witness in that she has a PhD in pharmacology, teaches at a university, and is highly respected for her scientific research. Dr. Benally recently led a series of studies investigating the side effects of the class of drugs that will be under discussion during the trial. She has served effectively as an expert witness in a number of similar trials over the last five years.

Dr. Josephine Rickman is a medical doctor who also has a PhD in pharmacology. She has a busy medical practice. Dr. Rickman sometimes serves as a medical news correspondent on a national news program. She is the author of three best-selling books on medical topics, including one on the pharmaceutical industry. Dr. Rickman prescribed the drug in question to a number of patients who appeared to have experienced side effects like those to be discussed during the trial.

WP-S097

Scratch Paper
Do not write your essay in this space.

LAST NAME (Print)

FIRST NAME (Print)

SSN/ SIN

L

LSAC ACCOUNT NO.

MI

TEST CENTER NO.

SIGNATURE

M M D D Y Y
TEST DATE

TOPIC CODE

Writing Sample Response Sheet

DO NOT WRITE
IN THIS SPACE

Begin your essay in the lined area below.
Continue on the back if you need more space.

EliteView™ forms by NCS Pearson EM-252259-6:654321   Printed in U.S.A.

COMPUTING YOUR SCORE

Directions:

1. Use the Answer Key on the next page to check your answers.

2. Use the Scoring Worksheet below to compute your raw score.

3. Use the Score Conversion Chart to convert your raw score into the 120–180 scale.

Scoring Worksheet

1. Enter the number of questions you answered correctly in each section.

	Number Correct
SECTION I................	_____
SECTION II................	_____
SECTION III..............	_____
SECTION IV	_____

2. Enter the sum here: _____

This is your Raw Score.

Conversion Chart
For Converting Raw Score to the 120–180 LSAT Scaled Score
LSAT Form 0LSN86

Reported Score	Raw Score Lowest	Raw Score Highest
180	99	101
179	98	98
178	97	97
177	96	96
176	—*	—*
175	95	95
174	94	94
173	93	93
172	92	92
171	91	91
170	89	90
169	88	88
168	87	87
167	85	86
166	84	84
165	82	83
164	81	81
163	79	80
162	78	78
161	76	77
160	74	75
159	73	73
158	71	72
157	69	70
156	67	68
155	66	66
154	64	65
153	62	63
152	60	61
151	58	59
150	57	57
149	55	56
148	53	54
147	52	52
146	50	51
145	48	49
144	47	47
143	45	46
142	43	44
141	42	42
140	40	41
139	39	39
138	37	38
137	36	36
136	34	35
135	33	33
134	31	32
133	30	30
132	29	29
131	27	28
130	26	26
129	25	25
128	24	24
127	22	23
126	21	21
125	20	20
124	19	19
123	18	18
122	16	17
121	—*	—*
120	0	15

*There is no raw score that will produce this scaled score for this form.

ANSWER KEY

SECTION I

1.	D	8.	A	15.	A	22.	A
2.	B	9.	E	16.	D	23.	E
3.	B	10.	C	17.	D	24.	E
4.	D	11.	B	18.	C	25.	B
5.	E	12.	E	19.	B	26.	A
6.	A	13.	B	20.	D	27.	B
7.	C	14.	B	21.	E		

SECTION II

1.	D	8.	A	15.	B	22.	C
2.	E	9.	E	16.	C	23.	D
3.	C	10.	A	17.	A	24.	B
4.	D	11.	A	18.	A	25.	D
5.	A	12.	A	19.	D		
6.	C	13.	B	20.	C		
7.	D	14.	D	21.	E		

SECTION III

1.	A	8.	A	15.	A	22.	B
2.	E	9.	C	16.	E	23.	A
3.	A	10.	B	17.	B		
4.	C	11.	D	18.	D		
5.	D	12.	D	19.	C		
6.	A	13.	D	20.	D		
7.	C	14.	B	21.	B		

SECTION IV

1.	E	8.	E	15.	B	22.	C
2.	B	9.	D	16.	C	23.	D
3.	A	10.	A	17.	D	24.	E
4.	D	11.	A	18.	A	25.	B
5.	C	12.	C	19.	E	26.	B
6.	C	13.	A	20.	A		
7.	E	14.	A	21.	C		

LSAT® **PREP TOOLS**

New! **The Official LSAT Handbook**

Get to know the LSAT

The LSAT is a test of analytical reasoning, logical reasoning, and reading comprehension, including comparative reading. What's the best way to learn how to approach these types of questions *before* you encounter them on the day of the test? There's no better way than The Official LSAT Handbook, published by the Law School Admission Council, the organization that produces the LSAT. This inexpensive guide will introduce you to the skills that the LSAT is designed to assess so that you can make the most of the rest of your test preparation and do your best on the test. (Note: This handbook contains information that is also included in The Official LSAT SuperPrep. The information in The Official LSAT Handbook has been expanded and updated since it was first published in The Official LSAT SuperPrep.)

$12 ($9.95 online)

LSAC.org